LEADERSHIP LAND MINES

8 MANAGEMENT CATASTROPHES AND HOW TO AVOID THEM

MARTY CLARKE

MARTIN PRODUCTIONS
Raleigh, NC

Published by Martin Productions
9660 Falls of Neuse Road, Suite 138-233
Raleigh, N.C. 27615

Publisher's Cataloging-in-Publication Data
Clarke, Marty.

Leadership land mines : 8 management catastrophes and how to avoid them / Marty Clarke. – Raleigh, NC : Martin Productions, 2005.

p. ; cm.
ISBN: 0-9769526-0-2
ISBN13: 978-09769526-0-2

1. Leadership—Handbooks, manuals, etc. 2. Management—Handbooks, manuals, etc. I. Title

HD57.7 .C53 2005
658.4092—dc22   2005928786

Book production and coordination by Jenkins Group, Inc.
www.bookpublishing.com
Interior design by Debbie Sidman
Cover design by Chris Rhoads

Printed in the United States of America
09 08 07 06 • 5 4 3 2

Acknowledgments

Ginny Hupp was the organizing principle. She saw how it all fit together before I did.

Alison Hodges is my excellent and patient editor. Every page of this book has Alison's fingerprints on it.

Dennis Clarke was the second set of eyes and the last line of defense.

Jane, Matthew, Katie, and Lucy are the reasons why any of this is possible, fun, or even worthwhile.

Contents

Preface

Before we get started, I have to tell you that this book abides by one Rule and makes one Promise.

Rule

Even though we're talking about leadership, which is an abstract concept, the rule for this book is: No theory, all practical application. You can get theory anywhere you like. You will not have to work too hard to find more than a few experts serving up their leadership theories.

Not me. This book was written from experience, and concerns itself with ideas and strategies that you can *apply*, not just ponder. The key words here are not "think about a theory," the key words here are "implement these behavioral modifications." Or, more colloquially, "avoid these land mines!" Once you do, you will begin making a positive impact during critical management decision points, and get yourself on the path to leadership.

Promise

I promise, I vow, that after we're finished, if you stack all my ideas on top of one another, they will not spell out a word. Nope. No way. Simply put, I tend not to trust the many professional educational experiences whose core teaching points magically spell out words like LISTEN! ADVANTAGE! or BUNDT CAKE!

It's not that I find those books, tapes, and classes entirely worthless, but whenever I find myself presented with that type of educational experience I can't help but feel that either:

A. The architects of the educational experience retrofitted their critical teaching points in order to create a clever mnemonic, which convinces me that some of what I'm experiencing is fluff. Or,

B. It just turned out that way. It's just an amazing coincidence that, when they completed their content, and perfected the instructional design of that content, someone noticed that the core teaching points of the material spelled out MANHATTAN! Well, I'll be.

Straight up, I do not believe that B has ever happened. It's always A. And since I am all about boiling things down to their most elemental state to allow anyone to implement an idea quickly and easily for maximum positive impact, I view the Clever Mnemonic Approach as being a tad disingenuous. As a result, when I'm faced with this approach I feel like somewhere along the line my time has been wasted.

I hate to have my time wasted.

And since I refuse to waste yours, I have articulated and ordered my strategies and ideas in the way that I think makes the most sense, and will be of most use to you.

Actually, this is the book I wish I'd read the day I got my first management job. In fact, this is the book I wish I had read at *any* time during the many years I spent in charge of sales, support, and staff teams. But this book wasn't available, so safe to say I had to learn my lessons; step on all the land mines myself.

I had pretty typical experiences through my many management assignments, from leading a single team to heading up an entire department. All that time I definitely had three things going for me:

1. I knew I didn't have all the answers.
2. I was always willing to accept advice and learn from my mistakes.
3. I wrote everything down.

And so I got quite an education. The good news is I was paying attention the entire time. I'm glad I kept all those notes because now, after careful consideration, I have boiled those notes and the lessons they contained down to the eight most damaging leadership land mines that prevent managers from emerging as true leaders.

Battle-tested, written from actual experience and with no tolerance for any strategy that cannot be implemented immediately, this book lists those eight land mines and how to avoid them. I want *you* to be the benefactor of all the lessons I've learned. I wrote this book for you, whether you are:

- A management newbie
- A seasoned department head
- A corporate CEO
- A business owner

or anything in between. You can read it and make some critical adjustments in your professional behaviors to yield immediate improvements in the quality of your leadership.

Introduction

Before we get into the leadership land mines themselves, there are two important concepts that we need to cover.

1. Think "Body of Work"
2. Managing the Situation and Leading Your People

Think "Body of Work"

Stop thinking job description or job title and start thinking body of work. Professionally, what body of work are you constructing? If you retire today, what professional body of work will you leave behind? What's the state of your current body of work? These questions are critical because leadership is not a one and done kind of thing. It's not a country where you get your passport stamped and you're in. Leadership has more to do with consistency than with victory.

Think of it this way: As of this writing, 39 Super Bowls have been played which means over 1,750 Super Bowl rings have been awarded. Now, compare that with the current number of members in the Pro Football Hall of Fame, which is just over 225. A Super Bowl ring marks you as having won a big game, but a Super Bowl ring is not a free pass to the Hall of Fame. It helps. It helps a lot. But it's not an automatic bid. Not even close.

This is because an induction into the Pro Football Hall of Fame, *any* Hall of Fame, is a reward for consistent excellence *demonstrated over time*. That induction rewards a body of work. A body of work demonstrating excellence gets you into the Hall of Fame and that's where I want you to focus your thinking, vis-à-vis, your demonstrated excellence in leadership. Stop thinking about your next promotion and start thinking about what body of work you are establishing.

Leadership is (or can be) that thread of consistency that you weave through every professional decision you make and action you take, no matter how big or small. Managers make a million decisions and each decision demonstrates leadership or it doesn't. These decisions and actions build a body of work. It is your body of work that is going to tell the tale, not your current title or the title for which you're aiming. I don't care what your business card says. Your title does not make you a leader. Your title may put you in a position to lead but that's about it. Your decisions, your actions, your body of work are what make you a leader. That's why, typically, leaders are said to have emerged over time rather than just appeared all of a sudden.

The good news is that avoiding the most common and most damaging leadership land mines will have an almost immediate impact on your leadership ability no matter how far along you are on your career path.

Managing the Situation and Leading Your People

Anyone with management responsibility has a tough job for many reasons, not the least of which is that managers live in two worlds. In any given scenario, there are exactly two challenges to which every manager, every leader must rise.

Every leader must manage the business situation at hand while *at the same time* leading and developing his or her people. That's it. The managerial universe gets no more complicated than that. Trust me, that is complicated enough. Both challenges are extremely important and there are numerous land mines within each of those two parallel universes. Just the ability to *separate* those two challenges can give you an enormous leg up.

Managing the Situation

Business situations come in all shapes and sizes. Projects need to be completed. Revenue targets need to be hit. Press releases need to be written. Bridges need to be built. Name anything you like. When the dust settles, managers are expected to have produced *results*. Managers exist because for many projects and goals, *teams* of people can often produce better and faster results than individuals, and someone must be in place to lead and direct the team. However, many managers get sucked into the soap opera of their team dynamics and lose sight of the bigger business situation. This is very common and very damaging.

The necessity of keeping the desired business results in clear vision will come up a few times in this book. However, the cardinal rule is this: Business before people.

The business before people rule brings clarity to most critical decision points. Even when you are staring right at your people, the business *results* need to be in the front of your mind. When the desired goals are clear and ever present in your mind, the soap opera tends to fade away.

Ask any auto racing enthusiast and he or she will tell you that the pit crews of those race cars go over every inch of their automobile looking for the slightest imperfection or inefficiency. Using everything from very high tech tools to their own hands, they constantly examine the car from stem to stern. They are always looking for drag. Drag is the deadly enemy of speed. These crews are looking to remove *anything* that will slow the car down in the slightest. The sponsors are paying for results. They are paying for *wins*.

In managing a situation, with a clear vision of the business results needed, a manager must act in the same way a racing crew acts. A manager must constantly review the systems, people, policies, practices, and tools being used in any business situation. Anything that is not helping is probably hindering and must be modified or even eliminated.

That is managing the situation.

When I finally latched onto the phrase, "business before people" my managerial life became quite a bit easier. There was no more good cop/bad cop. All critical decision points eventually became intellectual exercises rather than emotional ones. In fact, because I acknowledge that, I am myself rather an emotional person, I was often my own worst enemy in making wise decisions as a manager. When "business before people" became my mantra, I was able to separate my emotions from the task at hand easily.

In practical application, when puzzled by a decision a manager needs to ask the following questions in the following order:

1. What is best for the business?
2. What is best for this person/these people?

Asking those questions *out of order* is usually where most poorly thought out decisions get their start. Asked in the correct order, business before people, a manager has a fighting chance to make a wise decision. Sometimes the answers to those questions can be rather hard to swallow. But managers get paid to make tough decisions and swallow a bitter pill every now and then.

Leading Your People

I can think of very few professional experiences I have found more rewarding and enjoyable than those times when I had gathered the right people around me, creating a team who understood the mission and were motivated to generate results.

However, just like well-weeded, blooming gardens do not happen by themselves, neither do high-performing teams. Both happen because of consistent attention and tending. That goes for teams of staff as well as for teams of salespeople. Great teams do not happen organically. They happen because the leader has the presence of mind to *lead* the team, and not just float along with it.

Business comes before people. That much we've established and that's not going to change anytime soon. However, even though business comes before people, nothing is going to happen without a group of people working together to accomplish common business goals. And, as someone in a leadership position, you send a message to your team every time you make a decision.

The question of "What messages am I sending to my team as a result of this action/decision?" is *critical* to leadership because your people are paying attention to you.

Yes they are. Trust me on this. Your people are paying attention to you.

Oh, they might not be doing what you tell them to do. They might not be producing the results you tell them to produce. They might even be acting like people who are patently ignoring you. But they are paying attention to you.

Everything you do.

Everything you say.

Your employees are paying attention to your every move. Each of your moves sends a message that shapes their faith in you:

- Are you worth following?
- Are you worth listening to?
- Are you smart?
- Are you fair?
- Forget your credentials. Are you credible?
- Do I have confidence in you?
- Are you making a contribution?
- Do you have any backbone?
- Do you care?
- Do you have a hidden agenda?

The list is endless, but what it all adds up to is the most important question in each employee's mind:

- Do I trust you?

That's what you sign up for every day that you show up to work as a manager. The cold fact is you cannot *make* anyone follow your lead. Your employees might give it a go for a while, but without a pattern of behavior that inspires their confidence, the situation will disintegrate. This is why I emphasize the concept of your professional body of work. You have the power in your hands to shape your employees' faith in you simply based on the quality of your decisions and actions over time.

Leadership, when you boil it down, is a trust issue. In all things related to your leadership of your team(s), the constant attention to the health and welfare of that trust is everything. This is why the following two concepts are paramount in leading your people: consistency and conviction.

- Consistency of action and decision-making tells your team that you have a plan in place and that your head is in the game.
- Conviction tells your team that you believe in what you are doing and that your heart is in the game.

Consistency and conviction cannot be taught. They cannot be faked. Either you bring those to the table every day or you don't. There is very little middle ground here. When you act inconsistently, or you really don't believe in what you're doing or saying, you can bet your team can tell. Sometimes they know even before you admit it to yourself. So, when I tell you your employees are paying attention to you, I mean they are paying attention to your consistency and conviction.

Managing the Situation

chapter 1

Land Mine!

It's All about Me

This land mine rears its ugly head any time a manager's decisions and actions are NOT ruled by the needs of the business, but instead are ruled by that manager's intense focus on either personal recognition or his or her personal agenda, whatever that agenda may be.

Whenever either of those two things outweighs the needs of the business, the It's All about Me land mine starts going off. When it does, these actions and decisions truly paint the manager in an extremely poor light.

Personal Recognition

Let's start with the issue of a manager's need for personal recognition. For the record, it is the manager's job to focus on *giving* recognition rather than on *gaining* recognition. Unfortunately, early in a professional's career, when you are still trying to move up the ladder and make it *into* a manager position, and get a chance to display some leadership, you spend lots of time doing the best possible work and trying to get yourself noticed. There's no shame in that, by the way. None at all. At that point, it *is* all about you. Still, while that method usually works in getting you the job, it's rather a poor training regimen for becoming a good manager and eventually a great leader.

When you keep the focus on yourself, and the It's All about Me land mine detonates, the reason it goes off is because all decisions and actions are being made NOT with the business results in mind, but rather, in an effort either to bolster your image or, worse, make sure your image does not get damaged in any way.

Either way, if the critical needs of the business actually do get served in the process of glorifying the manager, it's only by coincidence and certainly not by design. This behavior, no matter how cleverly you think you have it disguised, is usually pretty obvious. Unfortunately, the people who spot it first are the people who report to you. The team can see it and your credibility begins to erode quickly.

Here's a real world example of a terrible defeat I suffered at the hands of a manager who embodied this aspect of the It's All about Me land mine. I am happy to report that while I suffered the immediate defeat, the story ultimately ends poorly for the manager who perpetrated this fiasco. That probably could have been predicted because the It's All about Me land mine very rarely brings happy endings for those who trigger it.

This story is called:

Dorothy, Mr. Fabulous, and My Big Promotion

Back in the mid '90's I had the greatest job in the world. I was a sales trainer, flying all over the United States teaching sales skills as well as technical topics to a nationwide telecommunications sales team. What a ride. The weekly drill was:

Monday
1. Fly someplace
2. Check in
3. Set up the training room
4. Eat dinner
5. Go back to the room and watch ESPN

Tuesday
1. Teach the training class
2. Enjoy hotel brewed coffee
3. Eat
4. Sleep

Wednesday
1. Teach the training class
2. Enjoy hotel brewed coffee
3. Eat (possibly treat myself to a nice restaurant)
4. Sleep

Thursday
1. Teach the training class
2. Enjoy hotel brewed coffee
3. Fly home

See? Now that was bliss. I'd probably still be in that job to this day had it not been for that job's two fatal flaws.

A. It paid next to nothing.
B. There was exactly no advancement possible inside the training organization. If you wanted to move up in the world, you had to get a job in a successful sales branch any way you could, do your time and get your shot at a management position.

The most sought-after job in the sales branch was the Field Marketing Specialist. If you wanted a sales manager job, becoming an FMS put you on a fast track. All of us trainers were angling for an FMS job in a high-performing sales branch, preferably in a cool city.

I combed the company job postings and soon I applied for an open FMS job in Washington, DC. Not only does the District definitely rank high on the cool-city meter, it was at the time one of the most successful sales branches in the nation. Unfortunately, the known world was applying for this spot for those reasons, and for the chance to work for Dorothy. The person to whom the DC FMS's reported was the Major Accounts Manager, Dorothy.

Dorothy was a wildly successful sales manager at the highest level of sales in the company. Dorothy was the real deal. She had a reputation for being tough as nails and impossible to spin. She was all business and her people loved her. She'd won every award there was to win and her W2 was the subject of much awed conjecture.

Therefore, I showed up in Washington, DC for my interview in my best suit, my shiniest shoes and with my A-game in hand. What I found out during my interview with Dorothy was that all of the legends about her were absolutely true, but also that she had a secret. It turned out that with a little encouragement, Dorothy had a riotous sense of humor and was actually a bit of a potty-mouth. We got along famously.

Two days later, I was in New York City teaching a class on the architecture of the equipment involved in high-speed data transmissions. Spellbinding if you do it right, trust me. In my hotel room, I checked my messages right before my older brother Henri came to pick me up and buy me dinner. There she was on my voice mail, Dorothy, explaining how much she enjoyed meeting me and what a great addition I was going to make to her team. She ended her message by telling me she needed me back in DC "early next week so we can fill out the paperwork and pick a start date."

I was electrified. I'd made it. Henri showed up at the hotel with my best friend from high school, Brother Beyer. That night Henri, Brother Beyer, and I drove way down into Greenwich Village and feasted on duck tacos and other assorted Chinese-Mexican fusion food at this place called ChinoLatino. We hooted and hollered and raised many flagons toasting my successful future.

Enter Mr. Fabulous. Keep an eye on our boy, he's going to jump on the It's All about Me land mine with all his might.

It turns out that Mr. Fabulous, the Branch Manager of the DC sales branch, was very happy riding the wave of Dorothy's success. In fact, even though it was widely known among the rabble that Dorothy and her team were carrying the entire DC branch on their backs, Mr. Fabulous was taking as much personal credit as he could. It was all about Mr. Fabulous and for a time there, it worked.

Mr. Fabulous was being considered by Executive Management for a coveted Regional VP job. Mr. Fabulous was making sure the execs knew that it was because of *him* the DC branch was leading the pack. His campaigning and bow-taking were endless. Everything he did and said was designed to make himself look good. He was stomping on the It's All about Me land mine and his behavior had already become an affront to the real heroes, Dorothy and her team.

It got so bad that Dorothy apparently started making a bit of noise that Mr. Fabulous might be overstating his involvement in the branch's success. Mr. Fabulous of course knew that was true but hated her for even *thinking* of upsetting his march into the VP spot. In time, they became mortal enemies living under the same roof.

Now keep in mind, the FMS's reported to Dorothy and, up until that point, the hiring and firing of FMS's for the branch was entirely up to Dorothy. Her track record in this regard was impeccable. Flying in the face of this success, disregarding the needs of the business, Mr. Fabulous decided to teach Dorothy who was boss.

Back in New York, I brought my class to a close and I checked my messages one last time before I hopped the train from New York to my home in Delaware. Unfortunately, I had one last message. Catastrophically, it was from Dorothy. I will never forget Dorothy's voice telling me that we may actually *not* be picking a start date when I arrived next week. Clearly, something had changed and now Mr. Fabulous wanted to meet me.

She was embarrassed. I could tell immediately that she was not happy about having to leave me this message, essentially reneging on her earlier verbal job offer. I took this as a bad sign. And indeed, it was.

A few days later, I was back, dressed and pressed in the Washington, DC branch. Mr. Fabulous met with me for about twelve minutes, during which he asked me about the classes I taught while he checked his e-mail. When he finally did look at me, it was to tell me that he would keep my resume on file but they were going to keep interviewing other candidates. He shook my hand and that was that. I certainly did not get the job. I was back on the road, training. Back at square one.

□ □ □

Now, what contribution I *might have made* to the DC branch had I been hired is immaterial, academic, moot, and otherwise not germane. The point of the story is that Mr. Fabulous jumped up and down on the It's All about Me land mine. He could not stand for Dorothy to get the credit for the branch's success so he started doing things to make sure she stayed out of the spotlight, so that he could get all the recognition. It was all about Mr. Fabulous. Instead of making decisions based on what was best for the business, he started making decisions based on what would and what would not pose a threat to his carefully crafted image.

Mine wasn't the only incident. From what I heard later, he really got out of control. Mr. Fabulous was so wrapped up in himself that he began to believe his own hype. He started making more and more bad decisions. The execs eventually grew tired of his grandstanding and, of course, he wound up losing Dorothy who transferred over to the Reston, Virginia office. Mr. Fabulous's reputation made it tough for him to attract a new Major Accounts Manager and soon the DC branch slipped from the top of the rankings. Mr. Fabulous's credibility was shredded.

What is the lesson learned? Simple, Mr. Fabulous tripped the It's All about Me land mine repeatedly; he made a lifestyle out of it, and it eventually brought him down. He had good people around him, his branch was performing, and he'd gained the attention of upper management. If he had just played it cool, if he had just shown an iota of maturity and allowed his people to get the recognition they deserved, I am confident that the execs would have made the assumption that he was the brains behind the operation. He was the man with the plan.

But Mr. Fabulous did not choose that path. He held onto that land mine for dear life and it ruined his professional credibility. Thus, executive management quickly lost faith in him. Actually, I am not entirely sure whatever became of Mr. Fabulous, but I do know he never did get that Regional VP slot.

It has been my experience that the executive teams, the men and women in positions of power in corporations are, for the most part, very bright people. If a department, a sales branch, or a team is performing well, the execs look to see who is running that team, who is the person behind the curtain. If a manager is way out in front trying to grab all the glory, those actions reflect poorly on that manager.

Personal Agenda

Ah, the universe of the small-minded. Once you are on the lookout for this flavor of the It's All about Me land mine, I believe you will be astounded at how prevalent it is in businesses large and small. When a manager lets a personal agenda rule his or her decisions, that manager has truly left leadership behind.

I came face to face with the horror of a manager's need to serve a personal agenda one day when I got trapped in a discussion between my beloved boss Spike and our VP of Information Services, Zelda. I was in Spike's office when Zelda blew in, all in a bunch. She hopped off her broomstick and plunked herself down in the chair next to mine. Apparently, one of her employees had done something and her head was spinning with rage.

The following conversation ensued:

ZELDA: That's it! Spike, this is it for him. He's done!

SPIKE: Are we still talking about what's his name?

ZELDA: Yes!

SPIKE: I asked around and from what I hear the guy has debugged every line of code in the billing system. Which is, by the way, held together with chewing gum and coat hangers.

ZELDA: Spike, programmers are a dime a dozen. He's got to go.

MARTY (CHIMING IN): Who we talking about?

ZELDA: Mitchell Cranepool.

MARTY: Mitch? You mean Mitch the Answer Man? That guy's famous. He can debug *anything*. He's a human can of Raid. Lays hands on the problem, and it evaporates. It'd be spooky if he weren't a great guy and all. I heard he can change your screensaver with his mind. Shrouded in mystery and yet friend to all. I love the guy.

ZELDA: Marty. You're not helping.

MARTY: Seriously Spike, there is *nothing* this guy can't fix network wise. Plus he drives an '85 RX7. Very retro.

SPIKE (TO ME): Can you shut up for like two seconds?

MARTY: And Rex *loves* him ever since he installed that wireless connection in Rex's office.

Zelda (trying to regain control): See Spike, that's my point. He just waltzes up to the ninth floor and starts installing stuff in the president's office.

Spike: Rex was asking for that wireless thing for three weeks. Had him down my throat on voice mail every day about it.

Zelda: But Mitch didn't even *ask* me. He just ordered the parts he thought would work and walked up to Rex's office.

Marty: Yeah, and installed the thing in like two minutes. Spike, check it out, Rex was so happy he gave Mitch basketball tickets on his way out the door. Not the upper deck loser seats. He gave him seats in the *box*. Chicken wings, hot dogs …

Zelda: See? This is what I'm talking about.

Spike: It seems to me that what you're talking about is this guy, what's his name again?

Marty: Mitch Cranepool. And listen to this, the guy never takes the elevator. What's up with that? Only uses the stairs. No one knows why. My theory is he figures it would …

Spike (to me): Shut up. This is me telling you to shut up.

Marty: No sweat.

Spike (to Zelda): It sounds to me like this guy's getting a little too much attention for you. You can't fire him because he's good at what he does.

Zelda: He went way out of policy when he ordered the part.

Spike: Noted. He also showed a little initiative and fixed a lingering problem.

Zelda: He walks around like he owns the building.

SPIKE: Listen, I'm tired of this whole topic. Last question, you want to fire him?

ZELDA: I at least want to write him up.

At this point Zelda kept going and going. There was no getting through to her because she had her "I Hate Mitch" agenda blocking what little business acumen she possessed. She didn't want to write the guy up because it was in the best interests of the company. She wanted to serve her own petty, small minded, hopelessly self-absorbed interests. Zelda was not, as we can plainly see, exhibiting any leadership. Mitch was a valuable employee. A little quirky, but certainly no loose cannon. Zelda could not see that.

So now, let's go to the It's All about Me land mine tote board and see how Zelda scored:

1. "Spraying Her Bile to Whomever Was Within Earshot"— She discussed a sensitive employee issue in a public forum.
2. "From Zero to Fired!"—She detested the guy so much she wanted him fired for a minor first offense.
3. "Blinded by the Agenda"—She was not recognizing that, on balance, Mitch was a very valuable employee.

Wow! She hit the It's All about Me land mine trifecta!

To my way of thinking, she could have avoided this land mine by dropping her own personal agenda, which would have allowed her to realize that she had a great employee who fixed a problem and that in and of itself would have reflected well on her. She could have patted Mitch on the head, recognized his initiative, and let him know that he will probably want to ask before he orders any more equipment.

Instead, she felt threatened by her own employee and reacted poorly.

This story actually does come to a sad ending. Because Zelda had been initially defeated in her effort to destroy Mitch, she wound up doing her best to make life miserable for him. About four months later, I heard Mitch had left our firm and taken another job somewhere. It was obvious to everyone in our building that Zelda had just run a valuable and popular guy out of the company. She jumped on the It's All about Me land mine and it wound up costing her department and costing her company a valuable employee. The worst of it was, she couldn't have been happier. She just couldn't see how serving her own agenda had hurt the overall mission of the company.

Avoiding the It's All about Me Land Mine

This land mine gets easier and easier to avoid once you make what I call, The Shift.

The Shift

That shift is simply this: You have to shift your mental emphasis from figuring out how to make *yourself* look good and serving your own agenda, to getting results out of a team that serve the business agenda. The business agenda has to guide all decisions and actions, including who gets the recognition

The shift is a lifestyle. At each critical decision point, a *choice* has to be made. Either you focus on doing the right thing for the business, or you focus on how you are going to be the one to take the bow and/or make sure your agenda gets served. Without the shift in place on a regular basis, leadership is not going to rule the day.

Making and then living that shift sounds easy, and most managers will tell themselves, "Hey now, I'm all about my people. I'm all about the results. I don't care who gets the recognition ..." Hmmmm, maybe. Unfortunately, it's been my experience that the It's All about Me land mine gets a ton of lip service but very few people live the talk. I believe this is because the shift demands two things:

1. A high level of personal maturity
2. The ability to ask yourself an ugly question

Personal Maturity

Personal maturity foils the recognition piece of the It's All about Me land mine. Personal maturity allows one to let go of the *need* for recognition. The need for recognition, the need for external validation of your worth, is a deep and powerful addiction. Strong is the pull of the dark side, hmm?

This addiction affects managers in direct inverse proportion to their own self-esteem. A manager with a strong sense of self-esteem, not bravado or overblown ego, just quiet, solid self-esteem, will usually not fall prey to this land mine.

Look at the managers in your own organization. If you identify a manager who regularly trips the It's All about Me land mine, think about that person's self-esteem. Usually, it is very easy to see past the act and realize that the person actually does not have a whole lot of self-esteem. But in order to ascend into leadership one must reject this recognition addiction and realize two very important things:

1. If your department, your team, or an individual who reports to you does an outstanding job and produces excellent results, you, the manager, *do* get the recognition even if you are not the one actually taking the bow. It's *your* team producing results. The need to take the bow is at the very core of this land mine. Resist it.

2. When you stop chasing recognition for yourself, the volume of work you and your team are able to produce will increase exponentially. Chasing recognition takes time and energy. If you don't worry about how you personally are going to get your name recognized for a particular achievement, you'll find you can devote that considerable energy to other things. The recognition addiction creates mammoth inefficiency in a manager. Once you free yourself of the It's All about Me land mine, you will begin to experience a great mental freedom, which is extremely valuable. If applied wisely, you can truly raise your ability to lead many projects at one time.

Asking an Ugly Question

The question I learned to ask myself when I was wondering, even in the slightest, that I might be straying toward this land mine in my decision making process, is simply this:

Is this a Marty thing, or is this a company thing?

As long as I am honest with myself, the choice is clear. Chances are it will be for you too.

What would have happened if Zelda had asked herself, "Why am I trying to fire Mitch Cranepool? Is this a Zelda thing or a company thing?" Well, had she answered herself honestly she'd have seen that it certainly was NOT in the best interests of the company to lose Mitch. An honest answer to this question could have saved her from driving off a valuable employee and also saved her from crippling her own credibility in the process.

Also, it has been my experience when observing managers who make a lifestyle out of the It's All about Me land mine that they just do not last long in any one situation, any one department, or any one company. The reason for this is simple: When managers focus on themselves, the needs of the business get left in the dust and that becomes obvious not just to their teams but to everyone else. Eventually, the It's All about Me Land Mine catches up to them and puts a serious dent in their ability to lead.

Worth Repeating

- Beware of being obsessed with personal recognition or the need to have your personal agenda served.
- Shift your focus off yourself and onto the needs of the business.
- Personal maturity is the antidote for recognition addiction.
- If you are ever unclear about how to respond to a situation, ask yourself, "Is this a you thing, or is it a company thing?"

chapter 2

Land Mine!

Managing to the Exception

If I could teach the world to sing in perfect harmony, I might.
Maybe. I mean, I'd have to consider the upside.

However, if I could cure the business world of setting off the
Managing to the Exception land mine, I would. I would do it immediately. I would not pass Go. I would not collect $200. I would not
wait for a whistle. If I could, I would cure the business world of the
most insidious leadership land mine roaming the business landscape.
My opinion is that this is the leadership land mine that gives corporate life a bad name. But believe you me; this land mine is just giant.
When I worked inside big buildings, clawing my way up the corporate ladder, I found managing to the exception was a disease raging at
an epidemic level.

The Managing to the Exception land mine gets triggered in
two ways:

1. Any time a person, or group of people allow an idea to be shot down because it's not perfect, this is "overt managing to the exception"

2. Any time a manager lets a matter of small consequence dictate decisions on matters of large consequence, this is "unconscious managing to the exception."

Overt Managing to the Exception

To find an excellent example of overt managing to the exception we need look no further than my son, Primo. Primo is at this writing ten years old. And, like most inquisitive ten-year-olds, Primo asks a lot of questions. A *lot* of questions. This is very normal for a boy his age and his mother and I encourage this behavior.

However, he is, as all ten-year-olds are, an incredible exception manager. Give Primo any answer and he'll use his considerable brain to find the exception to that answer. Typically, these sessions will come out of nowhere while he and I are driving and I am caught completely unprepared. For example:

> PRIMO (LOOKING AT ME IN MY REARVIEW MIRROR): Dad?
>
> MARTY: My man.
>
> PRIMO: Why did they invent money?
>
> MARTY: Money? Um, so we could buy stuff. Like food and vacations. Like um … like when we go to Disney World and we …
>
> PRIMO: No, I mean actual money. Like bills and stuff. Like a five-dollar bill.
>
> MARTY: Oh, well, you know, sometimes it's easier to pay for what you want with actual bills than with a credit card or a check. Like when we go to get ice cream and we …

PRIMO: Does everyone have money in their pockets?

MARTY: Um, no. Not everyone. But most people have a few dollars on them at all times.

PRIMO: What about people with no hands?

MARTY: What about them?

PRIMO: They can't use money.

MARTY: Well, true, it's harder for them to handle money I guess, but that doesn't mean they don't have any.

PRIMO: What about quarters and stuff? People with no hands can't use quarters.

MARTY: Well … I suppose coins would pose …

PRIMO: What about people who have no arms?

MARTY: No arms?

PRIMO: Blind people cannot use money.

MARTY: A blind person with no arms or two different people?

PRIMO: If a guy got hit with a freeze ray a robber could go up to him and take the money out of his pockets.

MARTY: Primo, listen …

PRIMO: I think money is a bad invention.

MARTY: It is not. Just because …

PRIMO: If you forget your money and leave it on the sidewalk, what happens?

MARTY: Do you mean is it likely you'll get it back? No. Money left on the sidewalk is kind of a lost cause.

PRIMO: I think money is a bad invention. Who invented it?

At this point Primo has made his case that the monetary system of America is a bad idea because it doesn't work too well for:

1. People with no hands
2. Blind people

3.   People with no arms
4.   People who get hit by freeze-rays
5.   People who leave their money on the sidewalk

See? Simple. Based on that, Primo is ready to toss the entire monetary system out and go hunt down and punish those who developed it.

Now, I use the Primo example for a reason. The reason I use the Primo example is because this type of reasoning is natural in a ten-year-old. In fact, I rather like it when Primo gets his exception manager engine running. I find it wildly entertaining and it shows me he's got a pretty creative brain up there. However, while managing to the exception is a good thing in a child, it is *not* a good thing in a manager.

Managers who manage to the exception usually get a whole lot of nothing done and usually wind up being nothing but a drag on everyone else's productivity. This is about as far from leadership as you can get.

Very early in my career, I had the glorious misfortune of being asked to participate in a cross-departmental task force that was asked to think up and implement a creative idea for "Employee Appreciation Day." During the meeting while we were all seated around the conference table, one inventive soul, a bright young lady I will refer to as Crystal Palace, hit upon the idea of deploying coffee stations on each floor right outside the elevators. That way, when an employee showed up for work they'd be handed a nice cup of coffee on the way to their cubicles, offices, work stations, rallying points, productivity centers, and other professional domiciles. Her idea was to bring in very good high-profile coffee, with cups, real cream, the works. She topped off her idea by suggesting we put VP's at each station to serve the coffee to our overworked employees and send them off to their desks with a nice "Thanks for all you do."

Upon hearing this, I awoke from a nice trip to the Bahamas I was taking in my head. I sat straight up. And my mind started racing with:

"Wow, that's a great idea. That works just fine. Cheap. Quick. Personal. Plus most of the people in the building do anything to avoid the wretched black death we have in the break rooms. People in this building take their coffee seriously. I know I do. Well done there, Crystal Palace. And look, we might get this wrapped up in time for me to get home by dinner ..."

Oh silly Marty. Oh Marty, Marty, Marty, such a fool.

In the nanosecond it took for me to sit up and throw a parade for Crystal Palace in my head, my happiness was shattered from across the table by someone from the credit services department, a grotesque and bitter specimen I'll call Nosebleed, who piped up with:

"Crystal, I love that idea. I do. I mean it's perfect. But some people like tea. And I don't think it's fair that we leave the tea drinkers out. So maybe we should go in another direction."

My mind explodes with hatred for Nosebleed. All the time she's explaining herself I'm thinking:

Hey! Genius! We have about 1,200 people in this building and about six of them drink tea. So we're going to throw this awesome idea out because it won't delight one half of one percent of the population? You, Nosebleed, are everything that is wrong with corporate environments.

Second, I can just tell I'm going to miss dinner. Margaret will be most displeased. And when I explain why it happened her mood will not improve.

And third, don't say you think the idea's perfect and then explain how flawed you think it is!

All this is swimming in my brain when Nosebleed's second in command, Unsightly Rash, jumps in with "Yeah, plus what about Eric over in the collections department? He drinks Mountain Dew. He drinks like a *gallon* of it in like a single day."

Slipping … drowning …

Safe to say we wrangled and wrangled for hours trying to find the perfect answer, which of course never arrived. There *was* no perfect answer. There was never going to *be* a perfect answer. But that's not the point. The point was what should have been a simple decision turned into an unproductive marathon of pain because of the Managing to the Exception land mine.

We eventually went with Crystal Palace's awesome coffee idea and it was a huge hit even though it was quietly boycotted by Nosebleed's department.

As you can see, overt managing to the exception kills speed, squashes creativity, and reflects poorly on the managers who embrace it. You cannot be a leader and an overt exception manager at the same time.

Habitual exception managers act as they do, shooting down ideas and finding every reason, no matter how small, why something *can't* happen for any one or combination of three reasons:

1. They are desperate to show how smart they are.
2. They have a hidden agenda.
3. They genuinely do not see the big picture.

Reason #1: They are desperate to show how smart they are

This theory gives these folks (folks like Unsightly Rash) some serious benefit of the doubt but I believe it is well placed. Sometimes, especially when there are some heavy hitters around the table, some employees in their desperation to appear smart start finding the exceptions to the good ideas.

There's this sort of "Aha! I've seen something no one else saw" type of exhibitionism going on. It shows they are concerned. It shows they are creative. Unfortunately, if this behavior gets reinforced, the employee learns to do it habitually and winds up hurting themselves over time.

Reason #2: They have a hidden agenda

This theory gives the exception managers (like Nosebleed) no benefit of the doubt and yet sometimes they don't deserve any. Sometimes an employee shows up to a meeting with an agenda that reads, "I'm going to be my usual cooperative self. But if (insert name) even opens his/her mouth I'm going to smash them to pieces." Now, it would be lovely if this agenda and those like them were printed and handed out during the meeting. But they are not. A hidden agenda is just that and they are very dangerous. Exception managers are often keepers of hidden agendas. Also, it has been my experience that rarely do these types of employees contribute ideas of their own.

Reason #3: They genuinely do not understand the big picture

Unfortunately, this is all too common. Sometimes an exception manager will offer up "Well, it won't work for this reason or that reason" and neither reason will have a material impact on the results for which the effort is being made. Do not be scornful when this happens. Do not throw heavy objects or otherwise harm the offending employee no matter how annoying their contribution is. These folks are not leaders because they are not letting the needs of the business be the gauge of what to leave in or what to leave out of a situation.

Unconscious Managing to the Exception

I don't know why I find these instances hilarious, but I do. Even when it happens to me. Especially when it happens to me. Sometimes managing to the exception can happen in a strange and unconscious way. Sometimes the tail wags the dog. Here are two quick stories to illustrate. Neither one is too grave, but they will illustrate how easy and how common managing to the exception can be. Sometimes it just sneaks up on you if you are not on the lookout for it.

Smiling Mike, the Walk-a-Thon and the T-shirts

A very ambitious guy, Smiling Mike, went all out and organized a seriously huge walk-a-thon through our neighborhood. Mine is not a small neighborhood. It is a massive collection of houses spread over a vast landscape. So anyway, Smiling Mike was raising money for some worthy charity and the walk-a-thon was launched.

Because I am civic minded, and because I dig Smiling Mike, I volunteered to be on the support team, helping him out on the big day. That morning, as the sky was slowly turning from grey to blue, we found ourselves with an entire parking lot packed with walkers. Who *were* these people and why do they walk great distances? I don't know, and I do not count myself among them, as I am devoutly sedentary. In the fullness of time, we got all the walkers tagged and set them on their way.

I was most pleased, not only because we'd gotten the event off without a hitch, but also because I was sitting on the curb in the shade instead of walking along the clearly marked path. I was content. Smiling Mike however was red-lining about the t-shirts. He sat down on the curb next to me.

MIKE: Dude, I have a *serious* t-shirt problem.

MARTY: What? Are we going to come up short? That's explainable. I mean the turn-out was huge. Who could have predicted that? This neighborhood is technically bigger than Bermuda.

MIKE: No, no, no. We have enough t-shirts. But I got these *extra* t-shirts that say "Event Winner" on them.

MARTY: So give them out to the people who come in first. Like a guy winner and a girl winner. Wait, do people *win* walk-a-thons?

MIKE: OK, so male winner, female winner. What else? I have six of these things.

MARTY: Sometimes people get a prize if they come in last.

MIKE: Yeah. Good. Male winner. Female winner. Male last place. Female last place. OK, two more.

MARTY: Two more what? Give those out and be done with it. The last thing you want to do is start giving out stuff and then have someone get up in arms that they didn't get a "winner" shirt.

MIKE: But I have *six*. We need six categories.

MARTY: But just give away four.

MIKE: You don't understand. I have six extra in the box.

At this point, I realized that the tail was wagging the dog.

MARTY: OK, you have six. Who besides you and me know this?

MIKE: About the six extra? No one. The guy threw those in for me for nothing.

MARTY: OK. The first rule of life is the audience never knows what you *didn't* do. If you give out four, no one's going to ask you about the other two if they don't know the other two exist.

MIKE: So give out four and don't say anything.

MARTY: Absolutely. You know how people get about t-shirts and stuff. The audience never knows what you didn't do.

□ □ □

Having talked Smiling Mike in off the ledge he did go forth and award four "winner" T-shirts and all was well. Can you see how Smiling Mike was letting the tail wag the dog? This is no great crime and sometimes it's easier for someone outside the situation to see it. You might think it's funny (and so do I) but this kind of thing goes on in corporate *all the time*.

Want another managing-to-the-exception, tail-wagging-the-dog story? Here's one from high atop world headquarters. My super team of sales and product trainers had re-written the entire "New-Hire Training" course. The coursework was contained in a manual and this manual was the model of economy and clarity. It was a thing of beauty and my team had really worked hard to make it that way.

The coursework manual hit my desk for edit and as soon as I signed off on it, the manual would go down to the copy center. I had made only a few cosmetic edits and sent it back to the team leader. In less than five minutes, the architects of the manual were in my office. The team leader, a young lady named Delaware, was accompanied by my administrative assistant, Doris. Doris had the manual in her hands.

> **MARTY:** Nice work on that manual. When do we get one back from downstairs?
> **DELAWARE:** We have to talk.
> **MARTY:** Sit.

They sat down in the chairs in front of my desk. How long was this going to take? These two look serious. And why did both of them need to come in and talk to me? Why couldn't they just e-mail me or leave a note at the steps of a monastery? Why do they need to come in and sit down? I'm doomed.

DELAWARE: OK, we can make almost all the changes you want.

MARTY: That's wise. Except for the part when you said "almost."

DORIS: That's why we're here. We can't split the third module into two separate sections. We have to keep it in one big chunk.

MARTY: We all know it works better in two sections. That's how we had it originally. Why did you combine it?

Now here we had a bit of a pause. My super-keen managerial Spidey sense was tingling. The cat was about to come out of the bag.

Finally Delaware spoke.

DELAWARE: We had to combine the original sections into one module to give us five total modules instead of six.

MARTY: And that would be because … ?

DORIS: Wheezer.

MARTY: Wheezer down in the *copy center*? Since when does she care? All she cares about is smoking sixteen cartons of cigarettes a day.

DELAWARE: OK, Mart, track with me here. We want the manuals to have a tab for each module. The tabs come in packs of five. So we either have to have five modules or break them into ten.

MARTY: Wheezer is dictating the instructional design aspects of my department? This is madness.

DORIS: It's either that or we have to split the modules into ten sections.

MARTY (SMILING): Because ten is a multiple of five.

DELAWARE: Don't make fun.

MARTY: We're making changes so the tab thing will work out evenly for Archimedes down there in the copy center? No chance.

DELAWARE: Look. We've talked to Wheezer. She said they can't have all these incomplete sets of tabs laying around so we have to have sets of five or ten. Then we escalated to Reggie.

MARTY: What did Reggie say?

DORIS: Never returned e-mail or voice mail.

MARTY: Hmmm …

At this point, I got a familiar feeling and that feeling has always defined me as a corporate employee. And that feeling is the one I get when suddenly I'm a stranger in a strange land. Sitting there in my office, with my own employees in front of me, I suddenly feel I'm on the outside looking in. And a voice inside my head whispers, "Does anyone else beside me think this wacko situation is funny?"

Obviously, the tail was wagging the dog. The copy center's obsession with tabs is the linchpin upon which training manual decisions swing? Please. But don't think this stuff doesn't go on every day. It surely does. Delaware and Doris were extremely bright people and they didn't *set out* to manage to the exception. Like I said, it just snuck up on them.

However, the key is to stop the bus somehow while it's happening and take a look at the situation in its entirety. Then you ask questions about why we're doing what we're doing. Do not be afraid that the answers might be ridiculous. Do not be afraid to find these answers somewhat amusing. But do not hesitate to step in.

Managing to the exception is a productivity killer. Watch for it. The next time you get asked to be on a committee or worse, a "task force," get ready to spot the exception managers. Even when you gather your team together to brainstorm for some ideas, you will find the exception managers come out of the woodwork and quietly gum things up until no ideas are being implemented because no ideas are perfect.

Avoiding the Managing to the Exception Land Mine

I have good news and bad news.

The good news is putting a stop to managing to the exception in a situation is as easy as taking a rock out of your shoe. The bad news is that you probably cannot banish this land mine forever. Throughout your career, you'll probably fight it pretty consistently in yourself and in group settings.

Let's stick with the good news, this land mine is easy to fix. I have become a life-long crusader against this land mine, I'm not afraid to battle it when I see it. I've broken down my private counterattack into four steps. If you keep these in mind, you will have a fighting chance of avoiding the morass, the non-productive sludge produced by the exception managers. You'll also avoid being one yourself. Here they are:

1. Pay attention to your radar.
2. Ask yourself, "Is this a deal breaker?"
3. Stop the bus.
4. Call it what it is.

Step 1: Pay attention to your radar

The fact is, even though you'd think the Managing to the Exception land mine is a rarity, it isn't. It is quite the opposite. I cannot tell you how many times to this day I run across it. Get your mental radar tuned for this frequency and if you even *think* you are in a managing to the exception situation, you probably are. It's that common. Also, once you start getting good at spotting this land mine you will also start to identify the repeat offenders and those who have unfortunately made a lifestyle out of it.

Step 2: Ask yourself, "Is this a deal breaker?"

This is the critical step. This is where your own judgment is the measuring stick. When your radar goes off and yes, you notice that you are, or someone else is managing to the exception the first thing you have to do is isolate the exception and ask yourself, is this a deal breaker? Is this issue, this exception going to have enough damage on our ability to achieve the desired results that it renders the entire idea useless? This is the critical question.

Sometimes the answer is going to be "yes, it's a deal breaker." For example, should you or should you not wear a seatbelt? Well, on the one hand, most times you get in the car and drive you don't get in an accident. However, what about that remote chance that you *are* in a car accident? Well, at that point a seat belt will probably help save you serious injury and maybe keep you alive. So, is it managing to the exception to wear a seatbelt every time you get in a car? Yes. That exception has enough of a consequence that it's a deal breaker. It therefore makes sense, in my judgment, to manage to the exception and wear a seatbelt.

Many, *many* more times in your management life the answer to "Is this a deal breaker?" is going to be "no." Should we change how we design the training manual because the copy center has a thing about the tabs? No. Should we invent an entirely new monetary system because of freeze rays? No. And believe me, those examples are easy. Sometimes you are going to have to sift through your mind weighing the options and the consequences of a particular issue. In these instances, keep the results in the front of your mind and let them be your guide.

Step 3: Stop the bus

So there you are, sitting in a committee meeting, or presiding over a team meeting, and your radar goes off. While the debate swirls around you, you decide that in your judgment the issue in question is actually *not* a deal breaker.

Well, here's where you either stake yourself out as a leader or you resign yourself to running with the pack.

Show a little leadership. Stop the bus. Speak up!

Now you don't have to go and throw lightning bolts down off the mountain. All you have to do is surface your line of thinking. Articulate yourself, that should be enough. Don't be surprised when a few folks leap to your side, breaking the groupthink, *following* you.

Words like "Hold on a minute …" or "Hey, let me ask a question here …" or any variations on those themes are acceptable ways to step in and assert yourself as a valuable voice of leadership.

Step 4: Call it what it is

If it's at all possible, my advice is that you actually use the specific words "managing to the exception" when you surface your concerns.

I do and it always has an excellent effect. For example, I might say:

> "Hold on a minute, to say our wireless sales are down in the southeast region because our product is, as you say, 'useless in Florida' is managing to the exception. Our coverage is spotty in Monroe County but beyond that, we're solid. Now don't hand me Monroe County as the reason we aren't hitting our numbers."

or

> "I'm confused. Are we not going to consider Key West as a destination for our recognition trip just because we think a few people might prefer a trip to the mountains? Help me understand how that isn't managing to the exception?"

In the second example, I illustrate a favorite tactic of mine, which is called "Play stupid if you have to." If you are in a delicate situation where maybe your boss, or someone you definitely do not want to offend starts leading the conversation down the exception manager path, often it is useful to surface your line of thinking by acting a bit confused and posing a question asking for clarity. I find the following lead-ins extremely useful in this regard:

> "Wait, I'm confused ..."

> "Help me understand ..."

> "I think you make a great point. But I'm not clear on ..."

You get the picture. The list goes on and on. All of these phrases, and those like them, are very non-threatening. You need these in those touchy situations when you have to show a little leadership and steer the conversation out of the managing to the exception ditch. Many are the times when I'm in a client's office and the situation calls for my leadership but I cannot afford to contradict the CEO right to his or her face in front of his or her staff. Openly contradicting the CEO is what we in the consulting world call very, very bad.

However, I get paid to lead the discussions and projects in the most productive way possible. So when my radar goes off, I am not above playing dumb if I have to.

I learned this tactic from an excellent mentor of mine named Jean Claude. I was on a committee whose charter it was to design and implement a recognition system for our corporate employees. During a critical meeting, I watched in horror as perfectly imaginative and practical ideas were shot down as unusable because they only addressed 98 percent of our employees. This went on and on until Jean Claude, our General Council who was sitting next to me, raised his hand and said very politely, but firmly "Help me understand something. Are we managing to the exception here? I think we are. A system that can apply well to over 90 percent of the employee base is worth developing. We're rejecting these ideas based on the exception to the rule. We're managing to the exception, which is actually counterproductive."

The room went silent for a split second, and then ... Zoom! We started making progress like you read about. Jean Claude's simple logic had defeated the exception managers. Vive le Jean Claude! Let's break it down:

Pay attention to your radar—Jean Claude's been around the block a few times. He was on the lookout and I think he saw this one coming a mile away.

Is it a deal breaker?—Jean Claude thought not.

Stop the bus—All he did was raise his hand and ask a question. Without melodrama, he showed leadership as he stopped the bus.

Call it what it is—The most important thing I learned from Jean Claude in that meeting is that the exception managers HATE the words "managing to the exception." Using those very words, he left them undone and got our meeting back on track.

The exception managers sometimes give themselves away by starting sentences with "What if …" and "What about …" Certainly, these people may have legitimate ideas that will render a decent idea unusable. They deserve to be considered and listened to respectfully. But when they are left to run wild, the exception managers can literally kill a department's, a committee's, or a team's creativity and production.

As a manager, you must always be on high alert to whether or not the decisions you make are managing to the exception or not. Watch for the Managing to the Exception land mine in yourself, in your superiors and watch for it on your own teams. And when you spot it, I want *you* to be the one who stops the bus. I want *you* to be the one who emerges as the leader.

Essentially, triggering the Managing to the Exception land mine is the enemy of leadership. But this land mine runs rampant. Do not be a party to it, do not initiate it, and stamp it out whenever you can.

Worth Repeating

- There is overt managing to the exception and unconscious managing to the exception.
- Most people manage to the exception because:
  - They are desperate to show how smart they are, or
  - They have a hidden agenda, or
  - They genuinely do not understand the big picture.
- Remember the four steps to foiling this land mine:
  - Pay attention to you radar.
  - Ask yourself, "Is this a deal breaker?"
  - Stop the bus.
  - Call it what it is.

chapter 3

Land Mine!

The Super Doer

The kitchens in most nice restaurants are pretty busy places, pots boiling, knives chopping, skillets simmering, people moving around all over the place ... I want you to get that busy scene in your mind. Now consider the head chef standing in the middle of it. The head chef stands in the middle of all that activity making sure the kitchen produces, correctly and to the specifications of the guests, a series of beautiful and delicious meals. Plate after plate: Ultimately, the head chef is responsible. The head chef is in charge of it all, but the head chef isn't *doing* it all.

Oh sure, the head chef is probably quite capable of cooking a lovely petit filet topped with lump crabmeat, asparagus and possibly some creamed spinach on the side. The head chef certainly has the ability to concoct a soup, construct a salad, whip up a nice polenta of the day: You name it; the head chef could probably pull it off in fine style. But if the head chef tried to *do* everything in the kitchen, or even do too much, what would happen? Right! The kitchen production would slow down to a crawl, and in short order that would mean a very empty, unprofitable, and eventually closed restaurant.

Then what do you have? You have the head chef sitting on the floor of the now and forever silent kitchen, exhausted, burned out, bewildered and wondering what went wrong.

What went wrong? Well I'll tell you, the head chef was jumping on the Super Doer land mine, and chefs who jump on the Super Doer land mine just do not last. They wind up broken, forgotten, and bitter. On the other hand, head chefs who stand tall in their kitchens and lead their crews to produce great food quickly night after night wind up well paid, well regarded, and, of course, well fed.

Pop quiz! In the above analogy, who are you? Yes! Spot on! Nothing gets by you; indeed, you are the head chef. Now visualize:

- Your team
- Your department(s)
- Your company
- Your to-do list

You are the head chef, baby, and never forget it. And, just as the Super Doer land mine is the enemy of the head chef, it is also the enemy of leadership. The Super Doer land mine will do you wrong and damage your ability to:

1. Hit deadlines
2. Deliver results on multiple projects and objectives
3. Produce results and deliverables *quickly*

Simply put, the Super Doer land mine goes off any time you spot a situation or issue that should be handled by a staff member but instead you jump in and resolve the issue yourself. Infrequent incidences of this are fine and may occasionally be necessary. However, when managers make a habit of jumping in and resolving issues themselves instead of having their staff do it, they unwittingly give up on the very concept central to proper and effective leadership—that is the concept that you are there to *lead*, to show the way to others, not to do everything yourself. If you could do everything yourself just as well and just as quickly as the team could do it, well, you wouldn't really need the team at all.

But you do need a team because more often than not, there is way too much work to be done for just one person to perform with adequate speed and accuracy.

When a manager jumps on the Super Doer land mine, typically it is with the best intentions.

"Whoops, we might miss the deadline. Better get in there and do it myself."

"Holy moly, the CEO personally requested this project, better do it myself."

"Jumpin' cats! Big customer. Lotsa revenue on the line here. Better handle this one myself."

Bang! Bang! Bang! Land mines going off all over the place. Lot's of doing and running around but not a bit of leadership to be found. The manager hits the panic button too soon and steps in just at the time when he or she should be showing a little backbone by delegating to an employee and then letting that employee do his or her job.

Now, before we go too far down the path on this one, let's make a distinction: The issue is speed. The distinction I want to make is between the manager's personal speed and team speed.

Yes, it can come in handy that a manager is adept at resolving issues quickly. But the measure of the manager is *not* in personal speed. The measure is in *team speed*. Team speed emerges when you begin to display the ability to get your team to deliver *multiple results,* handle *multiple projects* quickly and effectively. Attaining this ability is gold. Team speed is your ticket to success and advancement and the Super Doer landmine is the direct and mortal enemy of team speed.

In any given situation, a manager typically detonates the Super Doer land mine when that manager notices one or both of the following:

1. The first sign of trouble and delay, or
2. The gravity of the situation

The First Sign of Trouble and Delay

I know this may not come as a shock, but not every project, not every sales cycle, not every initiative hums along right on time. Sometimes those nasty old storm clouds start gathering in the distance and soon you start smelling delays and missed deadlines. It is at that point, where you either ascend to leadership or you swan dive onto the Super Doer land mine.

One of the most ineffective young men I've ever known was a young man named Cartwheel. Cartwheel was a VP in charge of install. That meant, once the sales team sold a customer, Cartwheel's department was in charge of getting the services installed and up and running so we could bill the customer scads of money.

Cartwheel must have had about 125 people working for him because we had about fifteen products and services we were selling at the time. What an empire. He had installers and troubleshooters as far as the eye could see. I mean it's not like this guy was short staffed. Forget having his own conference room, Cartwheel had his own *floor*.

In my opinion, Cartwheel's only obstacle to becoming a superb leader was his knee-jerk response to install delays. Even little ones. Cartwheel was, as we will plainly see, a super doer.

Cartwheel's job was, essentially, to ride herd over the entire install process and make sure things didn't grind to a halt. However, if he saw on one of his many reports that there was a slowdown in the install of product X, he would jump in there and start working the X installs *himself*. Now, you tell me, while Cartwheel was out there catching up on product X installs, what was happening to the installs of products A through W? Correct! They all experienced problems. While Cartwheel was installing orders himself, the many other things that demanded his attention started backing up. The entire install process would slow down.

Here were the negative effects of Cartwheel's super do-ism:

- Delayed revenue attainment for our company
- Upset customers
- Increased pressure on customer service
- Lost customers
- A very upset sales force that was losing faith fast

The sales force definitely started to lose faith in the company's ability to install the products they worked so hard to sell. I always felt that was the result that wound up doing us the most damage.

The hidden tragedy was that Cartwheel ran himself ragged and he didn't have to. All he had to do was spot those storm clouds brewing and give some direction to his people and let them work the issues. But he did not. He was a super doer and even though he usually left the building long after dark, burned to a crisp, and even though he was working extremely hard, he and his department never enjoyed a reputation for being anything but an inefficient mess.

Had he stood fearlessly in his massive kitchen and kept the kitchen humming by providing direction to his crew, kept it *producing*, well, my man Cartwheel would have been one of those guys about whom other people in our building would remark, "How does he *do it*?" And the answer would have been "Simple, he's a leader." But he was not. He was a super doer and the company suffered mightily for it.

One of the lessons we learn from the Cartwheel example is that when you experience a snag in one area of your responsibility you can create a damaging domino effect on other areas if you detonate the Super Doer land mine. This only happens *if you let it.* You may have to step in briefly but then once you unsnag the situation, then you need to GET OUT OF THE WAY AND LET YOUR PEOPLE DO THEIR JOB. (Whew! That felt good.)

The Gravity of the Situation

Sometimes a manager sets off the Super Doer land mine when a project request either comes from way on up the food chain or it involves a huge revenue opportunity. Either way, when the gravity of the situation starts to rise, so does the craving to forget you even *have* a team and just do it all yourself. I get it: The pressure is on and your reputation is at stake. But again, here's the choice: Show some leadership and direct your team to produce excellent results, or stomp on the Super Doer land mine, do it all yourself and risk having other initiatives suffer.

My wake-up call on this concept came while I in the passenger seat of a car driving home from a visit to our Richmond, Virginia, office.

It was late afternoon and the sun was setting across Interstate 95 when my boss Spike called me on my cell phone.

MARTY: Marty Clarke.

SPIKE: Hey chowderhead.

Ah, Spike is being openly abusive. Spike's in a good mood. Relief floods through my body.

MARTY: What's up?

SPIKE: How far are you from Raleigh?

MARTY: Um, I'd say we're still a good 45 minutes out. Of course, we could hit some traffic around …

SPIKE: If you hit traffic, call me. Otherwise, come see me in my office before you go home. You *were* planning on coming in to the building weren't you? Or were you going to run to your car, hope no one sees you and scam out early?

MARTY: Nope. I was gonna come up and finish the …

SPIKE: Yeah, right. I'm the one who believes you. Just come see me when you get in.

Hmm. 'Tis a puzzlement. Spike's obviously in a good mood, but the "come up and see me" is a red flag. Hmm …

I arrived in Spike's office and found him behind his desk. The president of the company, Rex, was across the room with his arms folded, leaning back against Spike's giant window.

REX (POPPING UP OFF THE WINDOW AND SETTLING IN A CHAIR NEXT TO ME): Mart-man! How was the trip?

MARTY: Virginia? We're in serious trouble. They're about four below headcount and when I asked to see the office's sales pipeline forecast, the branch manager looked at me like he was the president of Planet Clueless.

SPIKE: Yeah, we know we know. The guy's gonna be replaced by month end.

MARTY: Good.

REX: Listen, Mart, I don't have a lot of time here. We had this idea for a new program and we thought maybe you'd be a good person to run it for us …

Rex proceeded to explain that with the business climate intensifying and the company growing as fast as it was, we needed to hire a person whose entire job would center on staff recognition and morale. The employee survey had come back with very low marks in the morale category. The Chairman had seen the results and decreed that a staff position would be created to turn those low marks around. The Chairman wanted an update in thirty days. So the gravity of the situation was extremely high. My boss, his boss, and the Chairman wanted Marty to get this thing done.

MARTY: So you want me to hire this person into my department?

REX: Right.

MARTY: And create the program through which he or she would raise employee satisfaction and happiness through increased recognition etc. ... Kind of a corporate cruise director. A minister of fun.

SPIKE: Right.

MARTY: I'm all over it.

Then there was a brief silence while we all stared at each other and I weighed the propriety of asking the potentially dangerous, reeking-of-office-politics question rattling around in my head.

SPIKE: What?

MARTY: Nothing. I'm on it. I'm very excited to get the program up and going.

SPIKE: And ... ?

When in doubt, it was always best to shoot straight with Spike and Rex, as they were, at heart, regular guys.

MARTY: Well I think we both know, and you too Rex, we *know* down in Human Resources, JB's head is going to explode. Like kaboom! Clearly, this is a Human Resources function and when she gets wind of this she's gonna go mental. I for one will enjoy it, but *you* guys are going to have her up here on the ninth floor, rampaging. I've seen her in full flight before, man, it's *sick*. And this is definitely gonna set her off. I just want you guys to know that it's coming. And you should have your stun guns ready or like escape routes planned or something for when she shows up.

Rex: You leave that to us. Look, Mart, don't say anything OK, but the last place we want to put this is with JB. The Chairman wants an update and we can't wait four or five months to get this thing going. Plus, if she did focus on it, then nothing else in her department would get done. Got it? We need this issue resolved, we need it yesterday, and we need it done right. So just get it done.

Marty: On it.

Spike: This does *not*, however, excuse you from your normal job of getting out in the field.

Marty: Roger that.

Spike: Where you going next?

Marty: Next week I'm Tuesday-Wednesday in Atlanta.

Rex: Atlanta's a fun town.

Spike: Yeah, sounds like a total boondoggle to me.

Marty: Yes, it is a boondoggle. Instead of spending two days in our Atlanta sales offices, I'm actually going to a spa in a remote part of Georgia so I can take a two-day bath in a special mixture of kerosene, clam juice, and old radio parts. Supposed to be good for my skin.

Spike: You *would*, you little freak.

Marty (to Rex): Don't worry about Minister of Fun thing. I'm on it.

Rex: That's all I wanted to hear.

As I rode down the elevator, I was pleased of course but I was more interested in the big light bulb that had gone off in my head during that meeting. Spike had given me the answer. The big light bulb, actually more of a Vegas-style neon sign, was blinking in my head saying, "Get it done." It was not saying, "Do it." It was saying, blinking, and screaming the answer to success and advancement: "Get it done." They hadn't given me the project because of my sparkling personality. It came down to a question of *confidence*. It came down to who could get it done without making the rest of their department's results suffer. I was most pleased.

Also, I learned I had gained a reputation for running a get-it-done department. My department had a reputation for delivering multiple results, keeping "many pots boiling," and this more than anything had resulted in upper management's giving me more and more responsibility. I had team speed. This is the reputation you want.

The Super Doer land mine will gain you the *opposite* reputation. JB's reputation. The death knell for a manager comes when that manager's department or team gets the reputation for being *slow*. Delivering substandard results will just plain get you fired fast. But "slow" kills your credibility and your prospects over time.

When this land mine gets detonated in a sales environment, it usually happens when the gravity of the situation has to do with a large revenue opportunity. Sometimes when managers (usually rookies) start seeing the possibility of a significant win, a big sale, many times that manager will push the sales person into an entirely supportive role and try to land the account him or herself. Even if it works, and it does not always work, the rest of the sales team tends to feel quite resentful of all the attention they are NOT getting from the sales manager.

The cold reality is that the super doers are usually not happy people. After a while there is not a ton of personal satisfaction in doing everything yourself. In fact, it has been my experience that typically two paths lay ahead for any manager who embraces the Super Doer land mine:

1. Burnout ("I'm putting in too many hours.")
2. Resentment ("They just don't appreciate me around here.")

Burn out

This is an extremely unfortunate result of becoming a super doer. The insidious thing is that burnout does not hit all at once, it creeps in like water in your basement, slowly doing damage. Usually the damage comes in the form of substandard work, physical exhaustion, and personal unhappiness. This brings me to …

Resentment

After repeated detonations, the Super Doer land mine usually causes resentment. Resentment toward what? Resentment toward the company and usually toward direct superiors. Unfortunately, some folks who are resentful do not mind sharing it with anyone within earshot. Do you know any of these people? I do. These super doers are bitter, bitter souls who maybe had big aspirations and some initial success but then it all seemed to evaporate and now they are stuck where they are.

Once that happens, if the super doer does not change his or her ways and start utilizing the team, pushing authority out onto his or her people so they can flex their muscles and produce results, then the bitterness and jealousy starts to set in. You never have to actually articulate the sentence "They just don't appreciate me." If that is your attitude, your co-workers and superiors will smell that attitude on you. There is no masking it because it reeks.

Let me clue the super doers in on the answer to that statement: The reason they just don't appreciate you is because you haven't given them a reason to in a while. My experience has been that some of these super doers who fall into bitterness actually stay with their company for a long time. I think this is because they'd rather wallow in righteous indignation than re-invent themselves and make another run at being a leader of a productive team.

Avoiding the Super Doer Land Mine

The good news is that you can give up being a super doer in an instant. You will probably go through a bit of an adjustment with your people but it will be brief if you hold your ground. Actually, my suspicion is that your team will respect you more, and even enjoy working for you more too.

Here are two critical concepts in avoiding the Super Doer land mine:

1. When in doubt, ask yourself "Am I doing it or am I getting it done?"
2. Make the leap of faith.

Am I doing it, or am I getting it done?

This is a magic question. Ask yourself this question *regularly*. "Am I doing it, or am I getting it done?" I don't particularly care what *it* is. IT could be attaining sales quota. IT could be running the training organization, managing the research and development team, managing many projects, it doesn't matter. Whatever your discipline is, whatever results for which your department or position is held responsible, if you can make a habit of identifying your tasks and measuring them against this question, you should be OK.

If what you are *doing* could be delegated and trusted to an employee on your team, then delegate it. If this process is unfamiliar to you, congratulations, you are now on your way to becoming about 150 percent more efficient and thus more valuable to your company. You are on your way to becoming a leader.

> *Leadership is not being great; leadership is getting greatness out of a group.*
>
> MAX DUPREE

I want to share with you a trick I learned from a boss of mine named Madeline. Madeline: Now here was a shrewd corporate employee if ever there was one. Maddie was the first "remote manager" I ever had. She communicated almost exclusively by e-mail, made sure she followed up behind me to make sure I was providing tip-top training to the national sales team, and left me alone when I wasn't traveling. Since my reviews always came back very high, I made Maddie look good. Madeline had in her department about eight or ten trainers running around the country delivering training in the field. Also reporting to Maddie were the training class designers and schedulers. As you can imagine, with as complex a department as Maddie's, her list of to-dos was always extremely long and complex.

Madeline would avoid the Super Doer land mine by taking a giant yellow legal pad and drawing a straight vertical line down the page, splitting it in half. Down the first column, she'd list everything her department had to accomplish in the next 90 days (Madeline was a big "90-day" girl). She would include everything.

Big to-dos, tiny to-dos, urgent and otherwise, they all went down the left hand side in no particular order.

Then, next to each to-do, in the right hand column Madeline would put an X next to anything that she was doing or the name of the person to whom she'd delegated the responsibility. Too many X's was a serious red flag for Maddie. Also, she got a visual of another red flag and that was the question of whether or not she was overloading one person or spreading the work out as evenly as possible. Madeline rose through the ranks not simply because she worked hard, of course she worked hard, but she rose up quickly because she knew how to get things done.

Confidentially, I once saw Maddie get a bit fed up with a delay for her request for additional staff. So she made a copy of her legal pad page with her many and complex to-dos on it and she sent it to her Regional VP. Then three days later, she followed up with a polite phone call. What a shark. Of course, she got the necessary staff approved and went about the business of leading her excellent team. I definitely liked working for Maddie and I learned a lot from her. I wonder if she remembers me?

The leap of faith

Once you ask yourself the question "Am I doing it or am I getting it done?" And the answer comes back—"Well, I'm doing it and it should be delegated" then you have a choice. This is the choice that separates the leaders from the drudges-who-have-people-reporting-to-them. The leaders make the leap of faith. The leap of faith comes in when you pry your hands off a particular project/task/whatever and let your people do their jobs. Now, this *does* imply that you've recruited people to your team who are worth that leap of faith. But we're not going to talk about that now—in fact, that's probably a whole different book.

So, even assuming you have the right people around you, showing a little (and sometimes a lot) of faith is not easy at first. In fact, this is probably one of the most nerve-wracking moments in a manager's life. Your professional reputation may be on the line. The result of your decision might be on display for all your peers to see and judge. Trust me; making the leap of faith in your team is going to give you a little heartburn. It may give you a moderate anxiety attack. Do it anyway. Take the pain. Let your people do their jobs.

There's going to come a moment in time, a decision point when you will feel that panic, that knee-jerk urge to take over a project, to become personally involved in a particular task. It is in that very moment when you decide to become a leader or not.

> *'Cause if you lose your head and you give up, then you neither live nor win. That's just the way it is.*
>
> J. WALES

Perhaps you've made such a habit of being a super doer that you don't even notice this decision point. This is not tragic, but if you want to make an immediate improvement in your effectiveness all you have to do is get yourself off autopilot, be a bit more mindful, and try as hard as you can to take notice of when and why you are performing a particular task.

When you do, you will get better and better at it and soon you will be able to spot these decision points coming. When that happens, you can be prepared to talk an employee in off the ledge when an emergency hits, and make some suggestions on how THEY can resolve their issue. Sometimes you will need to get involved in some cursory way, kick open a door, get an approval signature from upstairs, whatever. The point is you get in there, remove the roadblocks, and send your people back in the game.

There's leading and then there's doing. Remember, leaders don't rise to power because they do a lot. They rise because they put their teams in a position to get a lot done.

After you've made a habit of making the leap of faith in your team and you've gotten to the point that you can keep an eye on many issues at once instead of working yourself to death being a one man or one woman department, you will begin to realize a hidden benefit. The hidden benefit is that you will develop what I call the Butterfly Meter regarding all your people.

The Butterfly Meter

The Butterfly Meter lives in your brain and on any given decision to delegate, the Butterfly Meter measures, with incredible accuracy, the number of butterflies that decision releases into your stomach. Every manager feels these twinges, but how many really pay attention to them and are mindful enough to keep track of who gives them the most butterflies and who on their team are the butterfly killers? Not many.

The Butterfly Meter can tell you quite a bit about each member of your team. It can also give you an edge on deciding who is best suited for which project. Let's take the example of a staffer I had working for me who for the purposes of this story we'll call Worker Bee.

Worker Bee was a young lady who was extremely capable when given very defined tasks with very defined deadlines and measurements. If I had to get a report written on the effectiveness of our sports marketing campaigns in Kentucky, North Carolina, and South Carolina, that was a Worker Bee job, no doubt. These are the graphs I want. These are the measurements. I need it on my desk for edit in four days. At this point, the task has been handed off and even though the president requested this report, my Butterfly Meter is delivering a very low reading. This is right in Worker Bee's wheelhouse.

On the other hand, let's say we needed to come up with a treatment for new sales contests and we had very little direction on the front end. Were I to hand this one off to Worker Bee the Butterfly Meter would go crazy. This would have the potential to blow the poor girl's mind.

Now we have an opportunity to play my favorite game, "Leader or Punk?" I have the sales contest project, I have no choices other than to do it myself or hand it over to Worker Bee. Hand it over to Worker Bee? Holy Anti-Depressant! All of a sudden, my Butterfly Meter starts going crazy. Whatever I do, my choice of action will reveal me to be either a rare and valued leader or a common punk who just happens to have people reporting to him. What to do, what to do …?

Now, let's play "Leader or Punk?"

1. I ignore the Butterfly Meter, drop the sales contest project on Worker Bee's desk and then, when she completely flames out, I complain how nothing gets done right if I don't do it myself.

    Leader or Punk?

    Correct! I'm a punk.

2. I pay attention to the Butterfly Meter and keep the project for myself, do a nice job, and walk around muttering about how I don't get paid enough to work this hard.

   Leader or Punk?

   Shaboomi! You are so right, I have punked out entirely and detonated the Super Doer land mine in the process.

3. I drop the sales contest project on Worker Bee. And because I know this will be a stretch for her, I stay a little closer in the loop and make sure she gets the mentoring and coaching she needs to help *her* bring the project to a successful conclusion, thus grooming her for bigger and better things.

   Leader or Punk?

   Wink Martindale's Ghost!* Three for three! You are correct. I'm a leader.

I've had the great privilege of having a few people work for me that were absolute butterfly killers. I knew that when I handed a project off to these folks I could take my eyes off them, no babysitting needed, and know they'd come back with excellent results. These folks are in my own Hall of Fame for the simple reason that they made the leap of faith not only possible, but enjoyable.

When it came to ranking in my head who were the keepers and who were the sweepers on my team, I always considered the Butterfly Meter in making those decisions.

As you can see, the Super Doer land mine is one of the most damaging to any manager's quest for leadership. Now, I'm

---

* At the time of this writing, Wink Martindale is actually not dead.

all for rolling up your sleeves and jumping in when necessary, but keep in mind that if you do that too much, if you panic and jump in every time, your team speed, your overall productivity, and your leadership will suffer.

Worth Repeating

- You are the Head Chef.
- This land mine is typically triggered by:
  - The first sign of trouble or delay
  - The gravity of the situation.
- This land mine usually leads to:
  - Burn out
  - Resentment.
- Ask yourself, "Am I doing it or am I getting it done?"
- Make the leap of faith in your people.
- Pay attention to your Butterfly Meter.
- Remember to get out of the way and let your people do their jobs.

chapter 4

Land Mine!
The Blame Addiction

Before we begin, I must recite a poem I have written, inspired by the Blame Addiction land mine. This poem is called:

> *"The Car Is on Fire"*
>
> *The car is on fire*
> *We should never have poured gasoline on the car*
> *I wasn't the one who poured gasoline on the car*
> *You should never have thrown lit matches at the gasoline-soaked car*
> *In the future, we should avoid setting the car on fire*
> *If we put the fire out, we can drive home*
> *Whoops, too late.*

The Blame Addiction land mine goes off any time managers spot a problem and then instead of getting the problem *fixed*, they spend valuable time and energy trying to find out who is to blame for the issue or how we'll all avoid the situation in the future.

In a time of crisis, every minute and every ounce of energy you spend on finding out who or what is to blame or positing theories about how we're all going to avoid the problem in the future is time and energy that you could be applying to resolving the very business issues currently plaguing you or your company.

In any challenge or crisis situation, the second you shift your focus from "Who is to blame?" to "Fix what's broke, resolve the issue" is the second you begin to lead. Watch for this in all aspects in your professional life. The minute a problem arises, even the *hint* of a potential problem, watch how many people immediately focus their energies on identifying who is to blame, marshaling their defenses so *they* do not get blamed, and offering learned suggestions for a brighter future. Once you start paying attention to this, you will be stunned at the number of professionals who trip the Blame Addiction land mine.

Some co-workers, you will notice, make a lifestyle out of the blame issue. Be advised, none of these people are exhibiting any leadership. None. They are common. They have no backbone. They cannot lead because they are small-minded. Possibly, you can tell that I have a very low opinion of these people. You are absolutely correct. I have no use for them. And if you were on my team, this place-blame, avoid-blame approach would give you the life expectancy of a housefly.

Let's take a look at a compressed example of the Blame Addiction land mine played out in a great movie called *Apollo 13*.

In this movie Tom Hanks, Kevin Bacon, and Bill Paxton play the astronaut crew of the ill-fated Apollo 13 mission to the moon. Kevin Bacon's character performs the routine chore of stirring the oxygen tanks and whammo! an oxygen tank explodes and blows out an entire side of the space craft.

This is what we in the space game call a very bad situation.

With the oxygen tank explosion not only are the astronauts not going to land on the moon, they might not even make it back to Earth at all. The cold fact is they might be stranded out in space forever, left to die a slow, agonizing death.

In a pivotal scene, they take stock of their situation. In the middle of it all Bill Paxton's character starts in on Kevin Bacon's character about how it's probably all his fault they are in this terrible circumstance. Tempers rise, shouting ensues, and then a leader steps in. Amid the din of accusatory shouting between the two astronauts, Tom Hanks' character puts a stop to it all and calmly but firmly explains that who is or isn't at fault is immaterial. It is moot. It does not matter because they have a problem to fix which, if they do not fix they are going to die. And he's right. Who cares how it happened? Who cares who's at fault? Every second they spend time and energy arguing about who is at fault is a second they are not fixing their problem. They need to fix the problem. Get the issue resolved. Every second they don't, they get closer to dying.

In the workplace, it can play out a bit more subtly. But it's there my friends. It's there. The best of them have learned to place and deflect blame so well that, as long as you are not paying attention to it, you never notice it. Consider this conversation, lifted from the very fabric of my corporate experience. This story is called:

Rex, the Emergency Meeting, and the Brokerage Firm

It was a gorgeous sunny day in October. The entire executive management team got called into our company president's private conference room. This was a great conference room because our president, Rex, had a small fridge installed in there and he kept candy bars in the freezer. But that's not important. So there we were, Directors, VPs, SVPs, and EVPs, sitting around the conference table all awaiting Rex's arrival. Oh baby, was it tense in that room. This was an emergency, all-hands, on-demand meeting. Everyone was looking around nervously wondering what we were doing there. Why had Rex called us all in? The odds of this meeting being very unpleasant were high, but still, no one knew what the situation was.

I knew.

Certainly, I wasn't saying, but I knew why we were there or at least I had a good idea. I'd been tipped off by a senior staffer of mine, Meredith. I'd learned long ago never to doubt Meredith and her endless supply of information. Meredith's prediction was that we were going to discuss the fact that a mammoth customer, Windfall Financial Services, had their entire data network go completely down the night before and here it was 9:45 am and they were still down. All fifty-five of their East Coast locations were down. About 600 brokers came into work that morning and could not transact any business with any client because their computers were entirely out of communication with all the major exchanges. No trades, no puts, no calls, no buys, no sells, no profits, no commissions.

No commissions.

Ouchie.

Windfall Financial was most irate.

They were:

- Losing customers
- Hemorrhaging revenue

We were:

- Losing significant revenue
- About to lose a significant customer

This is what we in the corporate game call a really, *really* bad situation.

So there we were, crammed into Rex's conference room.

REX (ENTERING THE ROOM AND CLOSING THE DOOR BEHIND HIM): OK. Who's not here?

DIRGE (CFO): Phil Welte's in Boca Raton. Other than that, this is it.

REX (SITTING DOWN): OK, clock's ticking folks. Windfall Financial Services' whole network is down hard. This is bad and every second it stays this way, it gets worse. We put out a press release two months ago when we signed these guys and right about now, we're costing them millions. We lose this customer, it's gonna be a huge revenue hit. Never mind that our competition is going to have a field day with this. Any way you look at this, it could be catastrophic. Dirge, tell them what we're up against here.

DIRGE: Well, I guess you could say that if we can't get Windfall back up in time, and we lost them as a customer, we'd have to restate our third and fourth quarter earnings to reflect the revenue loss. That's how big these guys are. Also, they'd more than likely come after us with a "lost revenue" lawsuit, which we'd more than likely lose …

As I stood with my back against the glass (I'd arrived strategically late so as not to get trapped at the conference table itself, plus I was right by the fridge) two thoughts occurred to me immediately:

1. Never doubt Meredith. Never, *ever* doubt this girl. Her powers of espionage were flawless.

2. Dirge was enjoying this. He was happiest when he was delivering bad news. If this guy ever got his dream job, it would be to count the dead at natural disasters.

So Rex cut Dirge off before he got rolling too hard. It was very clear. Every tick of the clock, money was draining.

REX: Restate earnings. Everyone hear that? Serious drop in profitability. That happens, we have to rethink a lot of things, a LOT of things: expansion, headcount, bonuses. Especially bonuses. No joke. We gotta fix this yesterday.

Yikes! As everyone let this sink in, the blamers emerged from the soil like the worms they are.

CARTWHEEL (IN CHARGE OF INSTALLS): That thing installed like a dream. Who was in charge of the disaster recovery plan? Because whatever the plan was, it ain't working.

JOE STYLE (NETWORK ENGINEERING): We should've waited until after October to upgrade the data system software. If we had done the upgrade in October, like I *said* we shoulda, we could maybe troubleshoot remotely.

REX: How about we talk about that later. Can we talk about *fixing* these guys?

THE HAMMER (EVP OF SALES): Look, whatever we do, we're gonna need to adjust the revenue target numbers. Without revenue from these guys, my team definitely does not hit quota and that's not gonna be *our* fault.

THE CONE (DIRECTOR OF BILLING): We ought to have ... like an alarm system or something. Next time a big customer goes down in the night we should all be alerted so we aren't scrambling like this.

Meanwhile, back at Windfall it sounded like this:

Tick, tick, tick, tick ...

No trades, no puts, no calls, no buys, no sells, no profits, no commissions ...

Tick, tick, tick, tick ...

DIRGE: Um, before this gets ugly ...

REX: It's *already* ugly. I got everybody working on the problem, I got no one working on the solution.

CARTWHEEL: If the disaster recovery plan had been in place, we wouldn't even *have* a problem. Who was in charge of that?

DIRGE: I like the idea of an alarm system. Are network alarm systems expensive?

When I tell you that this meeting raged in futility for about two solid hours, well, you just have to believe me. It was incredible.

Our customer was bleeding dollars and there we were, blaming, defending, pontificating, and generally getting nothing done. Ineffective does not even begin to describe it.

Toward the end of hour two of this blame-a-palooza, Rex, who was the only one wracking his brain for possible solutions, slipped me a note:

> "M, go call Patrick Hallway in billing. Look at the
> 120 day late-pays. Did we auto cancel Windfall?
> Tell him you'll hold."

So I did. See, Rex didn't care about blame; he wanted to fix the problem. The time to ask how and who would come later. The time to fix the problem was *now*.

Turns out he was right. I returned to the meeting with a note explaining the situation. Rex took the note and then looked up.

> REX (INTERRUPTING THE CURRENT BLAME-FEST): OK, everybody, cool it. We auto cancelled them. We shut them off.
>
> DIRGE: *We* did it?
>
> REX: Yeah, apparently, they've been paying us right on time but it's getting misapplied in our system, so the system shut them off for non-payment.
>
> THE CONE: Want me to call Richard Face over in accounts receivable and get him up here? This is his screw up. I mean not *his*, his *department* screwed it up. Personally, I really like Rich and all. I'm not blaming *him*, per se …

74

DIRGE: How can it be possible that our billing system can take down our biggest customer without us knowing it?

THE CONE: That's not *our* fault by the way. That's not the billing department's fault. Collections put that in there. Plus, we apply payments exactly how the sales guys tell us to.

THE HAMMER: Whoa, whoa, whoa, don't even *think* about trying to hang this on my guys.

CARTWHEEL: Problem's in billing. Billing or collections. One of those guys dropped the ball.

DIRGE: How much would an alarm system cost? I'm sure it's a significant expense and, just so you know, we didn't budget for anything of that magnitude.

REX: Who do I have to fire to get this customer's data network back up in the next five seconds?

In the end, Rex got fed up and sent his administrative assistant downstairs to go see Patrick and have him apply a temporary override. Unfortunately, it was going to be another three hours until we got Windfall Financial's network back in working order. Essentially, we'd cost them an entire day of financial transactions. Rex did not take this news well when his administrative assistant returned to the conference room.

REX: You're kidding me. What time is it right now?

MARTY: 12:15 pm

REX (PUTTING HIS HEAD IN HIS HANDS): Oh man, those Windfall guys are going to be livid.

If, when we gathered in the conference room early that morning, we'd have spent our time and energy fixing the problem instead of jumping like little demons on the Blame Addiction land mine, we may very well have gotten Windfall back up and running and saved them from losing an entire trading day.

We did not lose Windfall Financial that day. They stayed with us until the end of their two-year contract and then dropped us as soon as they could.

◻ ◻ ◻

Avoiding the Blame Addiction Land Mine

Use these four rules of thumb to help you avoid detonating the Blame Addiction land mine:

1. Identify the company pain.
2. Avoid being the town crier.
3. Should is your enemy.
4. Force yourself into present tense thinking.

Rule #1: Identify the Company Pain

This one is also called "Focus on the Bleeding, Not the Bullets." To illustrate this concept we need to consider my good friend, Dr. McKeen. As a physician working in the emergency room at a major hospital in downtown Philadelphia, Dr. McKeen treats all manner of violent inner-city injuries: People with gunshot wounds, people who get stabbed, people who fall into manholes, people choking on cheese steaks, Dr. McKeen sees them all and every last one of them is an emergency. I think that's where they get the name, Emergency Room.

Anyway, the point is, if Dr. McKeen steps on the Blame Addiction land mine, people die. Dr. McKeen has to focus on the bleeding (or whatever) and get the problem fixed. When the ambulance pulls up and rolls in a person who just got shot up with a machine gun, Dr. McKeen does *not* lean over the bleeding and broken, clinging-to-life victim and say, "Hey, nothing from nothing, but you mighta wanted to keep on the good side of the people with automatic weapons. Know what I mean? What did you do to irritate these people? Hey, no passing out, stay with me, I'm talking to you here. Lordy are you bleeding or what? Look at my floor. Listen, who was shooting at you anyway? *That's* the person oughta be in trouble right about now. Seriously ..."

No, Dr. McKeen does not do that. Dr. McKeen knows that there will be time for those questions later, but right now, there's a problem so she gets to work fixing the problem, getting the patient stable. Dr. McKeen focuses on getting the bleeding stopped. If she doesn't, if she detonates the Blame Addiction land mine, well the outcome is going to be tragic.

In times of business crisis, *you* are Dr. McKeen. You are the ER physician. Focus on the bleeding, find the company pain and fix it.

In the example of Windfall Financial Services' catastrophic data network failure, where was the pain? Where was my company feeling pain? The pain was *not:*

- Someone had blown the disaster recovery plan.
- We had no alarm system.
- We had in place a very powerful system that could shut off a client without our knowing it.

None of those things counts as actual pain. Those things were not the bleeding, although they may have helped us to identify them as possible bullets later on. During a crisis, focus on the bleeding, not the bullet. The pain was the loss of revenue and the threat of losing a huge client if we didn't get their network back up. Instead of stepping on the Blame Addiction land mine, Rex showed some leadership and went right at the money because that's where the pain point was. Since Rex zeroed in on the pain, he made significant and swift progress discovering a single point of failure that we didn't even know we had. That gave rise to new issues, but think about it, how much more time and energy would have been wasted by the blamers if Rex hadn't gone in and focused on the pain?

Rex re-established himself as having a cool head in a crisis and having the emotional maturity to forgo the bickering and sniping and get the central question identified and answered.

That is you. *You* are the one who is going to cut through all the noise and get the problem solved. You are going to zero in on the pain, fix it, and ask questions later.

Rule #2: Avoid Being the Town Crier

Try not to underestimate the acumen and awareness of your peers, superiors and staff. You do not need to be the Town Crier of what is obvious. But to this day, while working with clients large and small, whenever a particular situation reveals a person or a department had fouled up, there is never a shortage of folks who make it a point to make sure everyone knows where the fault lays. These are the "Town Criers."

Not only does this practice paint the Town Criers, accurately, as being rather petty and small minded, it also is an annoyance to everyone else who can probably figure it out for themselves. Town Criers are not leaders and no leader I've ever encountered brooked too much town crying within his or her own earshot.

Whenever a Town Crier stumbles into your cube, walks in your office, or corners you near the Snapple machine, bent on identifying where it all went wrong and who was at fault, my advice is to ask them, "What's your point?"

Try it. Pleeeeease. I want to know there are folks lobbing this one at the Town Criers.

Examine the following exchange:

TOWN CRIER: Can you believe they're delaying the order automation project *again*?

YOU: Yeah, that's a hurt.

TOWN CRIER: We were supposed to launch in May and now they're saying we're going to have to wait until August, maybe *September*.

YOU: Yep, that's gonna affect the year-end numbers for sure.

TOWN CRIER: Seriously. And let me tell you, Design should have been talking to Billing waaaay before now. I mean, come *on*. Order automation could be a miracle for us but if we can't bill it, then where are we? See what I'm saying? Am I right?

YOU: Hmmm …

TOWN CRIER: And that's JP Weathervane, you know. I mean I love JP, he's an awesome guy and he's great at what he does. But JP's the one who should have engaged The Cone over in Billing from the get-go. I mean that's his responsibility, right? JP Weathervane heads up Design.

YOU: Yeah, I know JP's department. What's your point?

TOWN CRIER: Point? The point is we're delayed. We're on our *second* delay.

YOU: Yeah, you said that. But what's your point about JP Weathervane?

TOWN CRIER: Nothing, I'm just saying.

Be advised, once the Town Crier pulls the "I'm just saying" ripcord, the conversation should be over. "I'm just saying" is business Latin for "I have no point. I'm just running my mouth for the sake of running it and it would probably be best for me to shut up and go work out my obvious self-esteem issues." My advice to you is this, remove the phrase "I'm just saying" from your vocabulary and avoid any conversations that might put you in a position to say it.

Asking the "What's your point?" question takes a little guts because it is a bit confrontational. Do it anyway. If you introduce this question, you will realize two important benefits:

1. It will immediately throw into harsh relief that the Town Crying is pointless, has no real business value, and is the corporate equivalent of high school gossip.

2. The Town Crier will typically make a mental note to remove you from his or her list of people who will listen to them blather on about who did what wrong. This is extremely important. As you take steps to improve your leadership, you must pay attention to the type of people that surround you. You do *not* need to be surrounding yourself with a bunch of blamers who are the biggest Town Criers going.

You hang around with nice people you get nice friends. You hang around with smart people, you get smart friends. You hang around with yo-yo's you get yo-yo friends. It's simple mathematics.

R. BALBOA

Rule #3: The Word "Should" Is Your Enemy

Simply put, the word "should" is the battle cry of the blamer. "We should have done that; we should never have done this." "Next time we should try and do this." When you are working out a problem and you have your team around you or you are in a group setting pay careful attention to the word "should" and to who is using it. These people are leaving the clues that they are blamers. Anytime the word "should" is used in any tense except the present tense as in "I think we should (name it) right now …" beware. The blamers are announcing their arrival.

Rule #4: Force Yourself into Present Tense Thinking

The blamers hate the present tense. They hate the here and now because the here and now demands action. In the face of crisis, blamers focus on the past and what caused the problem, and on how we're all going to avoid this situation in the future. Establish yourself as a present-tense thinker. As in, "OK, what can we do right now to address the problem?" The present tense is to the blamers what kryptonite is to Superman.

Back a few years ago I arrived in my home airport from an exhausting road trip. It was exhausting for a lot of reasons, not the least of which was that I was traveling with a career blamer who for his own protection I will refer to as Complete Waste of Space (CWoS). On top of that, I realized I was also working on a huge head cold. I could not wait to drop this guy off and get home.

However, the travel gods were not smiling on me and as I got to my car in the parking deck at 11:45pm, it became painfully apparent that my battery was dead. I put the key in the ignition, turned the key and got nothing. I tried about five times and each time the car was deathly silent. Sizing up the crisis, Complete Waste of Space started up with:

CWoS: Dead battery. That thing's deader 'n a doornail, boy.

MARTY (STARING STRAIGHT AHEAD IN DISBELIEF): Yep.

CWoS: Next time, you know what we oughtta do? Let's bring along one of those recharger things they sell in the hardware store. My brother's got one. That thing would come in handy right about now.

I just wanted to go home. I wasn't even going to take my suit off when I got home. I was just going to fall on my bed and die. None of what Complete Waste of Space was saying was getting me any closer to home at all. This guy could not think in the present tense, and thus he was contributing nothing to the current problem's resolution. Also he was aggravating me and sending my headache into the "eye-watering pain" category.

MARTY: Gimme your cell phone.

CWoS: Cell phone? Here you go buddy. Know what though? I betcha since they got this parking garage built up so close to the runway, the planes takin' off'll set off your alarm. And that'll run your battery down. I bet that's what happened. Next time, we ought to do that park-and-ride. It's free. You park way out by where the cargo planes are and they come by and bus you right in.

For the record, it is illegal to murder blame throwers who cannot think in the present tense. Do not, under any circumstances, murder these people.

MARTY (HANGING UP): Thanks.

CWoS: Who'd you call?

MARTY: See that sign? On the pole? That's the airport emergency help number. They said they'd have a guy over to give me a jump in twenty minutes.

CWoS: I bet he's got a portable jumper. You can get them in like Target, Ace Hardware, Home Depot …

I'm telling you, in the fury of a crisis situation the easy path is the talking path. It's easy to talk about what went wrong and what we can do to avoid it in the future. This path is also the ineffective, solving nothing path. Leaders take the harder path. They resist the instinct to talk and philosophize and instead do what they can, the best they can, right now. Leaders force themselves into present-tense thinking that leads to present-tense actions. Save the post-mortem for when the problem is indeed solved.

Sometimes, in the course of getting things done, someone on your staff may become a bit emotional and start to indulge themselves by stomping on the Blame Addiction land mine. If someone on your staff gets themselves going on a blame rant, it falls to you to interrupt the blame-fest or let it go. My advice is to step in. When you do, try using the following sentence to diffuse the situation and show some leadership.

"Your enthusiasm for what's wrong is evident. I know you have applied the same energy and enthusiasm to the possible solutions."

You commit this one to memory, and you'll find yourself in many situations when it will come in extremely handy. I learned this sentence when I was working in Florida. I heard it and then stole it outright from my old Florida boss, Tex.

I remember the first time I heard it. But first, a bit of geography:

We're talking about Tampa, Florida. If you look on a map, you will see that my beloved Tampa sits on the western edge of Florida. Curiously, if you draw your finger directly north you will see that lovely Tampa lines up longitudinally under places like Columbus, Ohio or Detroit, Michigan. That places Tampa near the westernmost edge of the Eastern time zone. Long story short, during certain times of the year, it stays light out well into the evening out there.

Back to business.

I remember it well, Tampa, 1995. I can see myself sitting in the conference room with my boss, Tex, a sales support rep named Molehill, and the manager of Major Accounts, Mr. Mustachio. I can recall my silent lament as I looked with longing out of the conference room windows. Here it was 7:45 at night and it was still sunny out. It was gorgeous. I knew if I just got up inexplicably and ran out, I could be on the Courtney Campbell Causeway in seconds and make it to Clearwater Beach in plenty of time to be on the beach to see what was sure to be a spectacular sunset. There I'd be, with my wife Margaret, and my newborn son, Primo, standing on the beach watching the Tampa sky turn from a radiant orange, to a livid red, and finally to a deep, deep purple. Then maybe we'd get banana milk shakes from the Dairy Kurl on the way home. Mmmmm …

But no, Molehill was still yammering on. I was trapped. He was in fact just getting his momentum going when my boss, Tex, stopped him in his tracks. It was a piece of leadership I have never forgotten and I've emulated myself on countless occasions.

MOLEHILL: … then install calls, *that day*, with a cut memo saying "well we can't provision this today because the D-Mark's been moved."

MR. MUSTACHIO: At the customer's request.

MOLEHILL: Right! We moved the D-Mark because they *told* us to. And I *told* install about it the day we did it, three weeks ago! Here, look at the e-mail. I printed it out.

MR. MUSTACHIO: So now we have …

MOLEHILL: So now we have the customer *waiting* for an install that's not going to happen and now everything's gotta be expedited and I'm sick of it. I'm *telling* you, I am sick of running around after other people's mistakes. My job is *not* cleaning up install's mess.

At this point, my boss, Tex, popped out calmly with this gem:

TEX: Your enthusiasm for what's wrong is evident. I'm sure you have applied the same energy to some possible solutions. So let's move on to those.

I stopped looking out the windows and turned my attention to the now stunned and entirely nonplussed Molehill. Mr. Mustachio had heard Tex drop this bomb in other situations before so he sat placidly while Molehill sputtered.

Let us review:

Your enthusiasm for what's wrong is evident. I'm sure you have applied the same energy to some possible solutions. So let's move on to those.

Did I log that one for keeps or what? And let me tell you, that one statement ended a useless blamefest/tantrum and turned it into a productive meeting.

It has been my experience that I never have to say that sentence to someone twice. If I drop the "Your enthusiasm for what's wrong …" bomb on someone, they usually come prepared the next time, which is good because the solutions are what we want. See? Let me clue you in, because I've studied these people. The blame people cannot take this. This one sentence makes them writhe in pain like that girl in The Exorcist. "It burns! It burns!" Keep in mind, the point is not to punish the blamers or hold them up for public ridicule. Tex did neither of these. The point is to lead the blamers out of the shadow of the valley of blame and deliver them into the productive promised land by casting out their blame demons or at least not indulging them. By saying this one sentence and refocusing our meeting, Tex did just that quickly and easily.

Blame addiction isn't like smoking cigarettes or overeating. People aren't walking around the business halls of America telling themselves they've got to quit one day. That isn't happening. In fact, just the reverse is true for many of your peers and your superiors. These folks, these small-minded souls have, regardless of rank, given up leadership in return for a never-ending quest to cover themselves in the face of any potentially damaging situation.

Think about it. You know who these people are. Some of them have gotten so good at placing and avoiding blame that their actions usually go almost undetected.

Almost. Now that you'll be paying attention, you'll begin to spot them and their methods. You'll be able to identify and then even anticipate their responses to these situations. That will buy you an immense advantage because you can then make the choice to separate yourself from them. You can assert yourself as a problem solver. You can emerge as a leader.

Stand apart and be thee separate! Count thee not among them! I'm sorry, but since you've read this far you have to show a little backbone. You cannot stand with the blamers anymore. From here on out you're going to have to ascend to that lonely position of a leader. The only upside is going to be the respect of your team and your peers, and your increasing value to your superiors and the company who employs you.

Worth Repeating

- The time and energy you spend on finding out who is to blame, or what should be done in the future is time and energy you could be using to fix whatever problem is in front of you.
- The four rules of avoiding blame addiction are:
    - Identify the company pain
    - Avoid being a Town Crier
    - Should is your enemy
    - Force yourself into present tense thinking.
- To diffuse a blamer on your own team use the following sentence: "Your enthusiasm for what's wrong is evident. I'm sure you have applied the same energy to some possible solutions. So let's move on to those."

Leading Your People

chapter 5

Land Mine!
The Popularity Priority

Whenever you make a decision based on what will make you more popular rather than what is best for the business, the Popularity Priority land mine goes off.

The Popularity Priority land mine is easily one of the most common, and most deadly, career-limiting land mines. What makes this land mine so very damaging is that when it gets triggered, you usually feel great without realizing that your professional credibility has taken a hit. Tripping this land mine once in a while is not going to hurt a manager too much. But when a manager starts tripping this one as a general rule, once popularity becomes the priority, the professional body of work is going to suffer. The credibility and respect damage mounts up until eventually, there is no coming back.

Think of it this way, if a generally fit and trim individual eats a nice slice of vanilla pound cake, the consequences will probably be minimal. However, if the generally fit and trim individual starts making a *habit* of eating slices of vanilla pound cake, the consequences are going to start revealing themselves over time. The Popularity Priority land mine is much like a slice of vanilla pound cake in the regard that the Popularity Priority land mine makes you feel great at the moment it goes off.

You trigger this land mine in the split second of a decision point. When you make a choice that seems pleasing or maybe just avoids pain, without thinking through the business and leadership consequences, the Popularity Priority land mine goes off silently and your credibility suffers.

Here are two examples; the first one is an example of how the Popularity Priority land mine can get triggered in a small decision regarding a single team member. And as we will see, sometimes a decision that seems small at the time can have large consequences. The first example is called:

False Face, Go-Kart, and the Vancouver Grand Prix

In 1997, back in the days when money was falling out of the trees for all the telecommunications companies, my sales branch won a national sales contest. The contest was for overall branch performance and since we won, my branch manager, False Face, earned a trip for himself and one other employee to magnificent British Columbia to get the VIP treatment and attend the Vancouver Grand Prix.

Now, who would False Face bring with him? Who would ride shotgun on this incredible trip, hobnob with Executive Management, get the trinkets, and otherwise bask in the glory that defines corporate recognition trips?

Me? I was not kidding myself. My team had performed well but our branch won because of the blockbuster performance of our major accounts team led by a real sales hitter named Candace. Candace was the major accounts manager and she had taken a middle-of-the-road sales team and in a very short period of time led them into the top of our national rankings.

So Candace gets to go to Vancouver, right? False Face will select Candace to share in this recognition event, right?

Wrong. Good answer, but wrong. Thank you for coming. Please drive home safely.

Instead of taking Candace, False Face took his best buddy, a guy in our sales branch who I will, with love, refer to as Go-Kart. Go-Kart was a known racing fanatic. Go-Kart was a nice enough guy, but he had made little or no impact on the production that led to our sales branch winning that contest. However, False Face didn't think that through. He just wanted to go with someone with whom he'd have a great time and who would be impressed with the trip itself. He hadn't thought through the fact that everyone in the branch would be outraged that Go-Kart was on a plane to take a bow for Candace's production. False Face just wanted to be popular with his friend and he figured he'd have a better time himself on the trip if he had Go-Kart with him. He had no perception that his credibility and respect would take a serious hit if he went that route.

Well let me tell you, the Popularity Priority land mine went off in a huge way. It was one of those things that everyone could feel but no one said out loud, unless it was a very private conversation. False Face took Go-Kart with him to the Vancouver Grand Prix and there was Candace back there with the rest of us.

Actually, I remember very clearly when our customer service manager, the much-beleaguered Patty stopped me in the hallway and asked me where False Face had been all week.

> **MARTY:** He's in Vancouver. He's at that recognition trip, at that race thing. He's got box seats, pit passes and the whole works.

Now here, Patty paused and looked a bit confused.

> **PATTY:** I just came out of Candace's office. Why isn't she in Vancouver, Mart?
>
> **MARTY:** He took Go-Kart.
>
> **PATTY:** Go-Kart? What's Go-Kart got to do with it? He took Go-Kart?
>
> **MARTY:** That's a fact.

At this point Patty just stared at me with her mouth open. Then her whole face changed into a very wicked smile as she shook her head and said something that decorum and good taste require I not repeat. But the sentence described how she thought that I must have been kidding her even though it was plain that I was not.

Now think about it. Candace was a high-performing major accounts manager and could have bought herself a few trips to Vancouver any time she wanted to. But that's not the point! The point is she got ignored and she new it.

And to Candace's credit, she never showed a bit of a reaction. She confided in me much later that at the time she was stung pretty badly by the incident. She was a true pro and never participated in any of the gossipy outrage that gripped the branch for months afterward.

While Candace never showed her true feelings, her team was going out of their minds with rage. They had bought her a toy Indy race car when they learned the branch had won the contest. But then there was Go-Kart home from the trip, showing off his pictures from pit row. What a mess.

I'm telling you, this one bad decision, based on popularity, cast a pall over the entire office. A pall to which False Face was oblivious. He was oblivious to it until months later when Vance, our regional VP came to our branch. I was actually in False Face's office when Vance arrived unannounced, closed the door behind him and asked for False Face's take on Candace's reasoning to move her family to Atlanta to take a major account manager job in that sales branch.

> VANCE: It's a lateral move. What's going on with this?
>
> FALSE FACE: Oh, um, bigger market, probably. Atlanta. Maybe she's grooming herself for a branch manager shot.

At this point Vance looked at me for a little help. I was no help at all and kept my mouth shut tight. Not easy for your humble narrator but I managed it.

> VANCE: Branch manager? She's on her way to that already.
>
> FALSE FACE: Maybe she's got family in …
>
> VANCE: Talk to me about the Vancouver Grand Prix. That came up when Candace and I talked yesterday, when she told me she was leaving for the Atlanta job.
>
> FALSE FACE: What? I didn't know she was a race fan. If I'd have known she …
>
> VANCE: It isn't about the *race*. It's about who got to go. It's the principle of the thing. You took Go-Kart. In fact,

at the post race reception, I couldn't believe you chose him. He's an analyst. I know he's your buddy but he doesn't even have a *quota*. Look at the trending reports. Candace was the reason you guys won.

FALSE FACE (GOING ON THE OFFENSIVE, HIS ONLY AVAILABLE STRATEGY): OK, so she's gonna leave the branch out of spite? Out of spite, she's going to leave the branch? Just because she didn't get to go on the recognition trip? C'mon. That's a bit much. That's like …

VANCE: According to her, this was definitely not an isolated event.

Now right here, we had what you call a pregnant pause. Finally I broke the silence with a curious but well placed:

MARTY: Just a question here, Vance. Is Atlanta in your sales region with us or is she gonna be over in Blonde Skeleton's region?

VANCE (STILL LOOKING AT FALSE FACE): No, no, we lose her out of the region. And that brings up a good point, False Face. What's the plan to replace Candace's production? Who do you have in the pipeline to replace her?

I made a dramatic move looking at my watch and said

MARTY: Hey boys, gotta bail. Conference call. You need me for this?

VANCE: Nope. Thanks Mart. I'll stop by your office before I leave.

Then I was gone, leaving False Face alone with Vance.

OK, I admit it. I wasn't entirely displeased with hurling a mighty spear at False Face at the precise moment when it would have done the most possible damage. Whatever, False Face was a punk and his lack of leadership cost him dearly. He had made a decision based solely on the premise of being popular, and in the fullness of time, it blew up on him. What leadership had False Face displayed? None.

☐ ☐ ☐

The second example is a little more subtle. In this example, the Popularity Priority land mine goes off a bit more quietly, but actually affects a large group of people. This story is called:

Go Ahead; Shoot the Messenger

Many times a manager will get marching orders from his or her boss that must in turn be made public to a team or some other group of employees. Sometimes these new marching orders are, to say the least, unpopular.

A manager is usually going to be able to gauge the audience's reaction to the new marching orders pretty easily. When I was the head of marketing, one of my department's responsibilities was to communicate company policies to the staff employee base, the sales force, and to the customer base. I was often to be found sitting at my desk with some new policy change to be communicated thinking to myself, "Oh boy, the sales team's not gonna like this ..." or "Uh oh, those folks down in customer service are going to riot when they see this ..."

Very few people *want* to be unpopular. Very few people *want* to be the bearer of bad news. I am no exception: I admit to feeling a twinge every time I readied myself to deliver information

I knew was going to be unpopular. Sometimes, in order to get information out quickly I had to deploy my entire team out into the field to deliver the news in person.

One such time we got the word that a certain sales bonus threshold had been raised and it was our job to take this news out to the sales force. In a nutshell, the sales team had to sell about 25 percent more widgets in order to make their monthly bonuses. One did not have to be a genius of perception to figure out how this one was going to go over.

We all saddled up, got in our cars, jumped on planes, and steadied ourselves to deliver the news. While I was on the road I got the news that one of my staffers was standing up in conference rooms, delivering the new bonus plan, and as soon as he was met with the requisite prison riot of sales people screaming at him and jumping up and down like little howler monkeys, he quickly side-stepped the wave of negativity by saying:

"Hey, don't blame me. I'm with you guys. I think it stinks too. I'm just here telling you what Corporate says. Don't shoot the messenger."

When I heard he was doing that, I was furious. Oh, I was red hot. My immediate response was to get this guy on the phone and burn him to the ground, with love, and make sure he never did it again. What a wimp! What utter lack of leadership! Then, as sometimes happens, fate lent a hand and my able assistant, the voice of reason, Doris called me.

> **DORIS:** Hi Marty, it's Doris.
>
> **MARTY:** Doris! Where's Jimmy Pence? Where did we send him? Can I just tell you …
>
> **DORIS:** Hold on. First thing, we need you to decide, *finally* …

MARTY: Because when I get my hands on that kid …

DORIS: On whether or not, Mart, are you with me?

MARTY: Go ahead.

DORIS: On whether or not you want to order the new graphics for the customer service brochure or go with the old ones.

MARTY: Customer service brochure.

DORIS: The *graphics*. The graphics for the new brochure. We either get the new ones ordered today or just use the old ones.

MARTY: I hate the old ones. The old ones have the old logo and whoever designed them used every possible shade of brown on those things. Brown's not even one of the company colors. And the fact that they *tried* to be creative but stuck to one color just kills me. They're all there, too. All the browns: tan, beige, sienna, burnt sienna, taupe, bark, ecru.

DORIS: So you want me to order the new ones or what?

MARTY: Suede. Milk chocolate. Mocha.

DORIS: Mart!

MARTY: Absolutely. Order the new graphics. These are the ones Gwen designed right?

DORIS: Right.

MARTY: I do love Gwen.

DORIS: We all love Gwen.

MARTY: Will they be done in time?

DORIS: Yes, we're good if we give Gwen the go-ahead on it today. Now, what's on your mind about Jimmy Pence?

MARTY: Jimmy Pence.

Doris: Yes, you're all up in a twist over something about Jimmy Pence. You said if you got your hands on him …

Marty: Jimmy Pence! Doris! Gimme his cell number. I need to get him on the line as of right now.

Doris: What's he done?

Marty: Never you mind. Safe to say it's about the new comp roll-out.

Doris: No problem. Let me get his contact information on my screen. Two seconds.

Marty: Good. Where is he, Jacksonville?

Doris: No, we sent the Glass Man to Jacksonville.

Marty: Hmmm, the Glass Man … he's solid. He wouldn't be standing up there going "Buh … buh … buh, don't blame me, buh … buh … buh …"

Doris: OK, here it is. But listen, Mart, maybe, you know and this is none of my business, but since we have the whole team in the field, maybe you could address this not only with Jimmy but talk to everyone at once and make sure everyone's doing the new bonus roll-out the way you want it. And then later, you know take Jimmy aside and well, whatever you want to do.

Marty: Conference call.

Doris: I mean, if you thought that was a good idea.

Marty: Conference call … yes … Because already it's what, 3:00 …

Doris: Yeah, so you can catch everyone before their after-market meeting and definitely make sure we start tomorrow all in lock step.

Marty: Lock step?

Doris: Sorry. Couldn't resist.

MARTY: How many people in this company make fun of me besides you?

DORIS: To your face?

MARTY: Never mind, set up the call. Let everyone know. I want all of them on the phone at 4:15.

DORIS: Done.

So we were all on an emergency this-means-you conference call at 4:15 and I let them know, without singling out Jimmy Pence (that would come later, privately), that I wanted everyone delivering this new compensation adjustment to show a little leadership, show a little backbone, and walk the company line. I told them if you genuinely do not believe this bonus adjustment is in the best interest of the company, call Ruth the Truth down in Travel Services and get on a plane home. No questions asked. Otherwise, you are the messenger, you are the voice of the company, you take the bullet. Stand in the fire and resist the temptation to embrace the Popularity Priority land mine. Take the bullet. It's for the good of the organization. You don't have to take any abuse, but you need to side with the company. Let them shoot the messenger. It has to be done. No one likes it. But show a little leadership out there. Anyone need Ruth the Truth's extension? Just say the word and you'll be home tonight.

□   □   □

It turns out that my team actually believed quite strongly that the new bonus plan was an excellent adjustment and the old bonus plan was in fact working against us, but that's not the point. Unpopular news needed to be delivered. The point is the Popularity Priority land mine was beckoning. And when it does, the pull to side with whoever is in front of you versus "corporate" is strong. I feel it. I like to be liked. I'd volunteer for the job of announcing we're all going to get giant holiday bonuses. But sometimes you get the job of delivering bad news or acting on an unpopular decision of your own:

- Holiday bonuses are cut this year.
- We have to work through the weekend.
- No more Friday "jeans day."
- You lose your office, you have to move into a cube.
- You have to take on more responsibility for no more pay.
- You no longer have a job here.

When you get the job of delivering bad news, you're going to feel the twinge and when you do you get to decide whether or not you're going to jump on the Popularity Priority land mine or not. And that split second decision can define you as a leader or as another person with "manager" on his or her business card who truly does not deserve it.

Avoiding the Popularity Priority Land Mine

So the question boils down to, "What do you want them to say?" Do you want them to say you were a great guy, or do you want them to say you were a true leader? Only you can ask that question of yourself and only you can answer it for yourself. I know, most people will say they want to be remembered or thought of as a true leader. Most people have those sincere good intentions.

But when it comes down to those decision points, those small choices you have to make every day as a manager, those are the times when lip service goes out the window and either you walk tall as a leader or you knuckle under, making sure you avoid being unpopular with your team or your audience. For those who want to avoid the Popularity Priority land mine, assume the responsibility, and act like a leader, I have two rules of thumb that have guided my managerial life:

- The Twinge Is Your Friend.
- Professional Distance Is a Good Thing.

By keeping these rules of thumb in front of you, you can make sound decisions when the Popularity Priority land mine is calling your name.

The Twinge Is Your Friend

Even though it can be very small, the twinge is extremely powerful. It is my position that the twinge is your friend. Earlier in this chapter, I spoke about the feeling most people get when they realize they have news that must be delivered and will probably be unpopular. It is during those times that most sane and socially adjusted people feel a small or sometimes large twinge. The twinge is that little voice inside your head that whispers " … they aren't gonna like you after this." This is the twinge that can make a manager hesitate, or worse, this twinge convinces the manager to do whatever is necessary to remain popular rather than doing what is right for the company.

Everyone feels these twinges and reacts to them. Exactly *how* you react is the leadership gauge. Once you get used to spotting this twinge when it hits, recognizing it, and respecting its power, the better you are going to get at reacting well to it. It all comes down to that decision point. Whenever I would find myself deliberating too long on how to deliver a certain piece of information or initiate a certain action I would ask myself if I was just avoiding being unpopular. The answer was almost always yes. Let me give you an example from the world of parenting. This story is called:

The Twinge, the Ice Cream, and the Job Chart

At this writing, my wife and I are raising three children below the age of eleven. We have a simple weekly reward system that says whichever child completes all the tasks on his or her job-chart (set the table, put your toys away, practice piano, etc. ...) that child gets a treat on the weekend. The treat is not substantial. Most times, it's a trip to the ice cream shop or to the bookstore.

Now, usually everyone completes their job charts just fine, but once in a while, one child will blow off his or her responsibilities. Whoopsi, empty job chart. That means no ice cream, no books, no whatever. When we see that, my wife and I feel the twinge in a large way. No one wants to alert a child that the two other children are going to the bookstore but, owing to the state of your job chart, you do not get to go. Plus, children who do not get what they want have a tendency to be quite demonstrative in voicing their displeasure, sometimes with their entire bodies.

I want an Oompa-Loompa right away!

V. SALT

When this situation presents itself, Mom and Dad arrive at a very common managerial decision point. It's time to show a little leadership, or pull the Popularity Priority ripcord. The choice may seem easy but it isn't. The twinge is calling up to Mom and Dad "Heeeeeeey ... C'mon now ... Don't be a buzz kill. You don't really want to tell her she can't go, now do you? Noooo. Plus, she's gonna hit the ceiling. C'mon, what's the big deal? Here's what you do: Tell her that she really needs to complete her job chart and that you'll let it slide just this one time. See? Everybody wins."

Oh, it is true! That nasty old twinge can make a manager (and/or a parent) really put on that thinking cap and get creative about how to avoid being unpopular. It's amazing what we can talk ourselves into. Let's say my wife and I feel the twinge and allow it to alter what we know in our hearts is the right course of action. We follow the easier, more popular path. We are sending a message to all our children that their job charts are actually not that important even though Mom and Dad say they are. We've taught them that even though we talk about consequences and responsibility, those things really don't mean too much when you get down to it. Also, Mom and Dad have reinforced the concept that whoever throws the biggest tantrum gets his or her way. The person who throws the biggest tantrum is in charge.

If our actions send these messages then this is not parenting. We're temporarily popular, but we're not parenting. We are definitely not leading. We're not leading because we've made popularity the priority. The same goes for management decisions.

If, when we feel the twinge, we stick to our guns and, with love, make sure that the child knows why she isn't getting this week's treat, we will probably have to withstand a tantrum, the odd "I hate you" and possibly a stomp up the steps. Certainly, we'll be pretty unpopular. But what messages are we sending now? We are sending a clear message to all our children that Mom and Dad mean what they say and their actions back that up. We send the message that Mom and Dad take this whole responsibility/reward thing pretty seriously. We also send the message that, even though a tantrum gets thrown, Mom and Dad are still in charge.

□ □ □

It might seem that the twinge is your enemy but exactly the reverse is true. The twinge is your friend because the twinge is the alert system that tells you that you are standing at a fork in the road and there is a choice to be made. Lead or shrink from your leadership responsibility. Each time you talk yourself into the easier, more popular path, the Popularity Priority land mine detonates and you risk damaging your professional body of work. So pay attention to the twinge when it hits. It can be your friend if you let it.

Professional Distance Is a Good Thing

The best managers for whom I ever worked understood the concept of professional distance. Even with the bosses who invited me to their homes for dinner, who took me to hockey games, and sent baskets to the hospital when my children were born, there was always the unspoken understanding that I'll articulate this way:

> *I'm your boss. I like you, I think you are great at what you do, and I enjoy your company. We're friends, but we are not peers.*

The key was that I knew and they knew we were not peers. This made our professional relationship work out extremely well. When I think about what traits my most valuable bosses had in common, this "I love you but we're not peers" idea ranks very high. With the bosses I wound up respecting the most, that line never got crossed.

Main Entry: peer
Pronunciation: 'pir
Function: noun
1: one that is of equal standing with another

Many managers shy away from this concept. I suppose these managers do not want to feel like they are holding themselves above their team members in some way. This is understandable. But the reality is, until a better system gets invented, there will always be managerial hierarchy.

Keep in mind, just because you and an employee are not peers does not imply any disrespect on your part. I've heard plenty of managers express the thought, "I don't want my team to think I feel I'm *better* than any of them because I'm the manager." Well that's a legitimate fear I suppose. Where is it written that just because you act like a leader you automatically feel you are inherently superior? It isn't written anywhere and it is entirely possible to treat every individual on your team with respect and kindness and still keep that all important professional distance.

Professional distance is maintained when:

- A manager makes and sticks to tough decisions regardless of how unpopular those decisions may be.
- A manager does not allow an employee to talk poorly about another employee, even behind closed doors.
- A manager does not allow an employee to complain about a situation unless that employee has also has solutions in mind.

Professional distance is destroyed when:

- A manager embraces the Popularity Priority land mine and avoids unpopular actions and decisions.
- A manager sides with employees in complaining about the company or other employees.
- A manager becomes intoxicated in front of his or her employees.
- A manager allows him or herself to become romantically entangled with a member of his or her team.

A quick word about the last two bullets. I am all for "bonding" events, team parties, and team outings. These events have a place in professional culture and, when done right, actually do make a team stronger and more effective.

However, that said, intoxication in any form or fashion is the mortal enemy of credibility. I was at a national recognition event once and witnessed my boss' boss get completely smashed at the opening reception. I never did look at the guy the same way again. None of us who were there did.

As for romantic entanglements, one would think it obvious that these would be lethal to one's credibility and sometimes one's career. I have personally witnessed five careers end because of this issue. All I'll say is that I feel anyone who takes their leadership seriously would do well to find romance beyond the walls of their own empire.

Guilt Throwers, Guilt Catchers, and Guilt Agnostics

There is another critical component that may prove invaluable in helping you avoid the Popularity Priority land mine and that is this: You must learn to spot the Guilt Throwers and the Guilt

Catchers in your professional life. I believe with all my heart that there are three types of people in the world: Guilt Throwers, Guilt Catchers, and Guilt Agnostics.

Guilt Throwers

These are the people who, in very subtle and sometimes overt ways, make sure you know they are the victims in any given situation. Their weapons are the rolled eyes, the sighs, the uncomfortable silences, and the pointed off-hand comments. Think about it for a minute and you'll realize there are many Guilt Throwers in your life. As soon as you identify a Guilt Thrower in your mind, that person loses 85 percent of his or her power.

Guilt Catchers

These unfortunates have latched on to the idea that, no matter what's wrong, somehow the fault, or some portion of it, lies with them. Underneath all the martyrdom, these folks are actually pretty self-involved. Think about it, they approach every situation with, "How does this relate to me?" The Guilt Catcher hates the idea of being the bad guy in any situation.

Guilt Throwers and Guilt Catchers tend to find one another over time and feed on each other. It's actually pretty depressing.

One of the biggest pitfalls for managers who are Guilt Catchers is they tend to skew their decisions just so the most potent Guilt Throwers will not react poorly. The Guilt Catcher must always be wary of trying too hard to be popular with the Guilt Throwers. What often happens is by tripping the Popularity Priority land mine in this way, one often trips the Managing to the

Exception land mine as well and then we're blowing up all over the place.

Guilt Agnostics

These well-adjusted individuals neither throw nor accept guilt and walk around wondering what all the fuss is about. The Guilt Agnostics do not mind the times when they have to be the bad guy. Guilt Agnostics usually have the best fighting chance of making a good choice at a decision leadership point and I would advise you to make every effort to migrate your thinking to mirror that of the Guilt Agnostics. This will put you in the best position to avoid the very damaging Popularity Priority land mine. If you want any shot at becoming a true leader, you must become a Guilt Agnostic.

Now listen up, about the guilt issue, this is how it all nets out: If you want to be a leader sometimes you have to be bad cop. When you do, the guilt throwers are going to come out of the woodwork and try to lay their guilt trips on you. Be advised, you do not have to comply. You do not have to accept and internalize the guilt, or worse, you DO NOT have to, in the face of a massive guilt storm, reverse field and go back on your original decision. That route can be catastrophic. Your only defense is to become a Guilt Agnostic and forever make that your management posture. Stick to your guns. Always. I'm not asking you to be a jerk, I'm asking you to be a *leader*.

What is your priority? Do you want to be popular or do you want to be a leader? The equation works like this. It's possible to make unpopular decisions and take unpopular courses of action that support the goals of the business and, over time, gain the respect of your team and superiors. It is in my opinion impossible to make only decisions you think will gain you popularity and wind up achieving any kind of success in the long run. The goals of the business must be your priority, not popularity.

Worth Repeating

- Making decisions based on your own popularity is like eating a slice of vanilla pound cake. It tastes good but if you make a habit of it, you're not going to like the results.
- Sometimes seemingly innocuous decisions wind up having huge consequences.
- The twinge is your friend, pay attention to it.
- Professional distance is a good thing.
- Guilt Agnostics are the only ones with a fighting chance to emerge as leaders.

chapter 6

Land Mine!
Cloudy Expectations

Imagine this: You are buying a new home.

No, wait. Strike that.

You've bought the land and now you are going to assemble a team of capable experts and *build* a home. Your dream home. *La casa de sus sueños*. Yes, glory is yours. Your home, your way. Every facet down to the smallest detail will reflect your remarkable taste and keen eye for design.

Now, what if all the people responsible for building your new home met on your empty plot of land and no one had the blueprints? There you are, standing with the painters, the carpenters, the masons, the landscapers, the plumbers, and the electricians and everyone grabs tools and gets to work without any blueprints. You tell me; would you or would you not be extremely nervous about the functionality and livability of your new home?

Of course, you would be nervous. Anyone would. So, if creating a blueprint of how you expect the house to be built is such an obvious first step, why then, pray tell, is the Cloudy Expectations land mine so very popular in the hallways of our own businesses?

The Cloudy Expectations land mine goes off when assumptions get made about how things are supposed to turn out.

What results are we after?

What are the consequences that arise when these results do not occur?

Not only does the Cloudy Expectations land mine create massive inefficiencies, but it can also cause hard feelings among the staff.

Back to your doomed house. Let's say you did show up and nobody had blueprints, but they all dove in and started banging away. Who would be the first person for whom you'd be looking? Correct, the General Contractor. The General Contractor is the person on any home building project who is ultimately in charge of that home being built correctly. It is the GC's job to deliver the expected result: a safe and attractive new home.

So you ask around and it turns out that the GC isn't there but should be dropping by later in the week. He's probably bringing the blueprints.

In your panicked misery, a few unpleasant questions are going to evince themselves in your desperate mind:

- How much work is going to have to be *undone* as soon as the GC gets here?
- What is the cost of the time and energy everyone has wasted?

- What is the cost of the heartache?
- If the contractor had the blueprints, why didn't he or she review them studiously with all involved *before* they started?
- Why are we now suffering when this could have been avoided so *easily*?

So, bringing this story to its logical and miserable end, the GC shows up eventually, and is horrified that the project is going in about fifteen wrong directions. The GC brings everyone to a grinding halt, and when the team looks around they see that not only have their efforts been wasted, but they are all now in worse shape than they were when they started. Everyone looks at the General Contractor and regards him as an incalculable chucklehead. Then everyone looks at you, the customer, with pity and says, "Looks like you're spending the holidays in temporary housing."

Why do General Contractors use blueprints?

Because blueprints are the expectations, down to the last inch, of how any particular house or building will be built.

Why do orchestras use sheet music?

Because sheet music illustrates the exact notes the musicians are expected to play so that pleasing harmonies and beautiful melodies are achieved.

Why not do the same for your team? One ribbon of consistency ran through all the *best* bosses I've ever had in my career, and that was that each of them made his or her expectations very clear. I knew exactly what was expected of me and I had a clear idea of the results I was to produce.

Let me relate a quick story about a situation where, as you will see, expectations were NOT delineated.

A few years back, my oldest brother, Maurice, treated himself to a gorgeous black automobile from a prominent German manufacturer.

Now our Maurice lives quietly but when he goes, he goes large and let me tell you this car had more electronics on it than the Mach 5 and the Stealth Bomber combined. Picture the four of us Clarke boys, Maurice (oldest), Henri (next oldest), Marty (classic attention-seeking third child), and David Dark (youngest) all standing outside, looking over Mo's new machine:

> MAURICE: Want to know something strange about the car?
>
> HENRI: What?
>
> MAURICE: Well, as you know, this model comes with the navigation system.
>
> MARTY: Wicked.
>
> MAURICE: Indeed. And for all I know, it works like a charm.
>
> DAVID DARK: Dude, you haven't used it yet? You drove it all the way from *Boston.*
>
> MARTY: Cambridge.
>
> DAVID DARK: Oh, yeah and Cambridge is like so far away from Boston. Thanks.
>
> MAURICE: Well, we tried to use it. I drove and Portia had the manual out but …
>
> MARTY: Hold it. You built a terabit router in your basement outta spit and Kleenex. How'd you get foiled by the navigation system in your own car?
>
> MAURICE (THE MODEL OF PATIENCE): We did not get foiled. See, the navigation system renders your exact latitude

and longitude. Within six feet, it tells you your exact latitude and longitude.

DAVID DARK: Satellite, dude. It's getting that from satellites.

MARTY: Really? I thought it was getting it from the navigation pixies inside the dashboard.

DAVID DARK: Which one is longitude? The equator is longitude, right?

HENRI: What good does knowing your longitude and latitude do you? Are you telling me that it has no map interface to tell you how that information relates to where you are?

MAURICE: Exactly.

DAVID DARK: So it's useless.

MAURICE: Largely, yes.

DAVID DARK: What's our latitude and longitude right now?

MAURICE (BENDING INTO THE DRIVER SIDE WINDOW): Um … 40 degrees north by 74 degrees west.

MARTY: Cool.

MAURICE: Yes, cool but useless.

The designers of this automobile jumped on the Cloudy Expectations land mine pretty hard somewhere in the design phase. Somewhere along the line, somebody said, "Hey, the navigation system needs to be accurate and fast." What they forgot to say was, "It needs to help people get from one place to another so make sure you build in a mapping function."

So that never happened and a very nice car got produced with a navigation system that doesn't do anyone without an advanced sailing degree any good.

The Cloudy Expectations land mine goes off any time a manager sets a project off in a particular direction without setting clear expectations of the people participating or of the project itself. The Cloudy Expectations land mine is the enemy of acceptable results. If the offending manager gets results anywhere near acceptable, then it was luck. If a manager knowingly leaves results up to luck, my thesis is that manager will meet his or her professional end sooner than later.

Avoiding the Cloudy Expectations Land Mine

I went to college seventy-six miles away from the house in which I grew up. I believe this is the perfect distance from home for any college student. Door to door, I was about ninety minutes from my parents' house. Now that's far enough away so that my parents didn't just "drop in" on me unannounced, and close enough for me to get home on the odd weekend to do my laundry and look malnourished enough for my dad to hit me with a few dollars.

For the most part, my parents left me alone on college hill, but I remember vividly the day they dropped me off at school for the very first time. My Dad made himself pretty clear. My family was back in the car and they were all set to leave me to begin my college adventure when my Dad drew me aside and the following conversation ensued.

DAD: How's your money?
MARTY: I'm good. I'm good. Mom gave me a few and I have Grandpa's fifty.

DAD: Good. OK listen up now, for the next four years, as long as you're in school, you call me every Thursday in my office.

MARTY: Thursday.

DAD: Collect. You call me collect in my office on Thursdays.

MARTY: Got it.

DAD: I know you got it. But I'm telling you, Marty boy, if you don't call me on Thursday, I'm calling *you* on that Friday. You hear?

MARTY: Absolutely. Call you collect on Thursdays.

DAD: Or I'm calling you on Friday. And if I don't get you Friday, I'm coming back here on Saturday.

MARTY: You're coming here.

DAD: In a heartbeat.

At this point, my father and I locked eyes and I realized that he was quite serious.

Let's review my Dad completely destroying the Cloudy Expectations land mine:

1. Call him Thursday or he's going to call me Friday.
2. If he doesn't get me Friday, he's showing up on college hill on Saturday looking for me.

That, dear reader, is an example of setting clear expectations. And, with simple instructions like that, I don't think I missed a Thursday call and my folks were able to sleep soundly knowing I was OK. My Dad exhibited excellent leadership in that he let me go my own way but set the clear expectation on how he was to remain in the loop on a weekly basis.

In any leadership situation, expectations must be clearly articulated in one or all of the following areas:

- Conduct
- Reporting and Feedback
- Outcomes and Deliverables
- Consequences
- Budget

Conduct

If a child acts in an obstreperous or disrespectful manner, most people will agree that the child's behavior is reflecting rather poorly on his or her parents. If an employee conducts him- or herself in a similar manner, the reflection on the manager is not quite as direct but it's close enough.

You need to make very clear what is and what is not acceptable in terms of how your employees conduct themselves. Now, of course there are a few accepted rules of professional conduct that pretty much everyone knows:

- It is poor form to throw sharp objects at other employees.
- Swordplay is frowned upon.
- No mixing bathtub gin on company time.

Beyond the above, consider this, how do you want your team to act at the big trade show? How about the holiday party? How about the recognition event? The team outing? How about everyday around the office? Leaving conduct up to chance is a pretty dangerous game.

Let me tell you about a very specific standing rule I established for the team members who would travel with me to trade shows. The rule was simply, if you show up to the booth and I think you are hung-over, you go home. Then when I get back to the office, you and I discuss your future as an employee. If I think you're hung-over, my next call is to Ruth the Truth in Travel Services back at headquarters. She will get you a ticket and you will be flying home that very day.

I set that expectation in the pre-show meeting for every show we attended. I told my team I could care less if everyone else in the company limped onto the trade show floor clutching a large coffee and sweating spontaneously. Not us. And that was that.

And so, with that conduct expectation established, I never had anyone show up (noticeably) hung-over. But more importantly, it set the tone for the rest of the event.

Occasionally, if the situation demanded it, I'd let a team member know how *I myself* was going to conduct myself throughout a particular project. I did this so they would know what to expect *from me*. This only happened when I assigned a particular team member a sensitive project and I could tell that I was going to be jumpy about it until he or she was through.

On those occasions that I could tell my conduct was going to stray away from my consistent pattern of behavior, if I were going to be a bit more hands-on than normal, I'd let the team member know in advance. I would tell the team member that until this thing got done, "I'm standing on your neck."

Pause a minute and soak in the visual …

Yep. This is me standing on your neck. When you look around, you will see me:

- Calling you for updates
- Watching my e-mail like a shut-in
- Haunting your cube
- Allowing you to use my home phone number
- And basically hounding you until you produce what I want and need you to get done

Since this was a rare occurrence, my team tolerated it with aplomb. I think the bigger lesson is that I told them, "This is how I'm going to act during this process. Usually I'm pretty hands-off, but now that you have this particular project on your desk, I'm standing on your neck." They were prepared and then didn't freak when it happened.

Setting clear expectations on conduct may seem like it falls into the "that goes without saying" category and I suppose sometimes it does. Even though it might "go without saying," I said it anyway. I never left it up to chance and I advise you to do the same.

Reporting and Feedback

One of the greatest expectation follies, and something sure to trigger the Cloudy Expectations land mine is the assumption, "If (insert employee/group) gets stuck, they'll let me know." That assumption is just plain not true and I learned it the hard way a few times. What I learned was the rule is, "If they get stuck they'll more times than not just stop and busy themselves with something else."

Even though I had a pretty good track record of hiring smart and talented people, I learned that unless I laid out what type of updates I wanted and when I wanted them, my team would be content to chug along on their own. A team chugging along on its own is rather like an ocean liner setting out to sea and no one has a hand on the steering wheel. The chances of either one reaching its proper destination are slim.

Outcomes and Deliverables

When I was working my days away in my beloved Tampa, the chain of command went like this: I reported to Tex, and Tex reported to the branch manager who was a tall Clint Eastwood looking guy to whom I'll refer as Jimmy Shotgun. Jimmy Shotgun was, by reputation, a hardliner with a flair for publicly humiliating anyone who was stupid enough to get too full of himself or herself.

He was also an extremely likeable guy who, if you did your job and produced what was expected of you, would treat you just fine. Jim expected results and results were what Jim usually got. In fact, I had only been assigned to the Tampa branch for three months when I noticed that we were on our way to hit our twenty-fourth month of exceeding sales quota. Two solid years. This was, in the eyes of the entire Tampa sales and service team, quite an accomplishment and certainly cause for celebration.

I surfaced the idea of a celebration to Tex and asked him if he'd take it up to Jimmy Shotgun for his approval.

It was right there in Tex's office that I learned a lesson about outcomes, deliverables, and clear expectations.

Tex told me that there was very little chance of that celebration ever getting approved simply because Jimmy Shotgun had set the expectation a long time ago that exceeding sales quota was our job. That's what we do. That's what he expected. If we'd hit a 200 percent month, Jim was all about celebrating. But consistent revenue attainment was our job and as I would later hear Jim himself say, "We're not going to throw a parade just because we're doing our job."

I may have been in the minority but I kind of admired his point of view and the backbone it took to send that message to the sales office. I have always remembered it. Let's listen to it again, shall we?

"We are not throwing a parade just for doing our job"

J. SHOTGUN

What expectation is Jim setting? Is he being clear about what outcome he expects or what? Now think about it this way: Maybe, the Tampa branch was such a consistent producer *because* Jimmy Shotgun was so crystal clear in his expectations.

Consequences

Consequences can be positive or negative. Positive consequences are pleasant experiences like more money, trips, and promotions. Negative consequences are unpleasant experiences. It is my opinion that not too much needs to be said on positive consequences simply because it has been my experience that most managers and organizations are actually pretty adept at setting up reward systems. It is the subject of negative consequences that I feel needs a bit more discussion and so that is where we will focus our attention.

Negative consequences should never, never come as a surprise to anyone. But so many times, they do.

Main Entry: con·se·quence
Pronunciation: kän'se-kwens"
Function: noun
1: something produced by a cause or necessarily following from a set of conditions

Consequences can come in many forms. Here are a few examples:

- You do not get your quarterly bonus.
- You have to work late to finish the project on time.
- You miss the Yanni "Under The Stars" concert this weekend because you'll be here working.
- You are fired.
- You have to go to Lakeland, Florida, for a week. In August.

In the practical world of business, a consequence is what happens to you as a result of you not producing the expected result or deliverable. Sometimes the consequence is you just have to stay at work and gut it out until the work gets back on track. Sometimes there is no work-around and the consequences wind up being financial.

All of that may sound obvious enough, but I think it needs to be pointed out simply because so few leaders ever lay out the consequences of falling short of the expectations they may or may not have made clear.

Then when things go, shall we say, kablooey, and all is darkness and hate, when projects miss deadlines, sales fall short, revenue does not show up, basic codes of conduct are ignored, when expectations just do not get met and consequences fall, well, if those consequences were a surprise, we just went from bad to worse. Now we have no results, and the failed expectations are now compounded by indignation.

Let me offer an example of excellent, clear expectation setting and listing consequences so that they come as a surprise to no one.

I speak of my oldest daughter, Artista's, second-grade teacher, whom for the purposes of this story I'll call Mrs. Ringo-Rango. Artista adores her and so do my wife and I. So, when Mrs. RingoRango asked me to give a little speech to her second-grade class I gratefully accepted with enthusiasm.

When I arrived on the appointed day, I arrived to an empty classroom. Mrs. RingoRango and her crew were just coming back from art class down the hall.

In those moments of silence, I took a look around and I noticed a sign on the wall that listed for one and all to see:

Behaviors
1. Feet on the floor
2. Hands to yourself
3. Kind words or no words

Consequences
1. Reminder
2. Loss of 5 minutes recess time
3. Loss of 10 minutes recess time
4. No recess/Note home to mom & dad

What could be clearer? See, Mrs. RingoRango doesn't mind being a leader. She says, "Here's the deal kiddos, here's how it's going to go." Then when the consequence hits, it is a surprise to no one. She combines these expectations with a simple reward system for good behavior and so, predictably, Mrs. RingoRango has very few discipline issues in her class.

Now I understand we as corporate leaders do not have the luxury of posting a sign every time expectations and consequences get set. Too bad. Here's the news: Leaders don't have signs so leaders *are* the signs. Leaders realize that in an expectation vacuum, bad behaviors and sloppy deliverables result. A garden untended will grow a few flowers, but mostly it'll grow weeds. The leader must articulate positive AND negative consequences.

Budget

The Cloudy Expectations land mine can also cause massive inefficiencies when a manager initiates a project without any budget in place to guide the spending of company dollars to complete it.

Now I know what you're thinking, you're thinking, "Mart, no way. Please. Now you've gone too far. No budget? This is madness. Crazy talk. Work a project without a budget? That just plain never happens."

Um, yes it does.

How about, yes it does and with *remarkable* regularity.

Without a clear understanding of spending expectations and limits—a budget—the people who are responsible for bringing a project to successful fruition are always having to guess at what resources should and should not be accessed. Then, because no one wants to be on the other end of the interrogative sentence, "You spent WHAT?" most employees usually resign themselves to waiting for approvals for every little expense related to a particular initiative.

This is how the Cloudy Expectations land mine gums up the whole process and causes inefficiency. Instead of doing a little thinking on the front end and creating a clear budget which lays out spending expectations, some managers (it's true!) will say something along the lines of:

> **VISIONARY:** OK people! We need (insert bold initiative) and we need it in sixty days. This is critical so let's really do our best work.
>
> **EMPLOYEE:** Please sir, what's the budget?
>
> **VISIONARY:** Budget? We, uh, well keep me in the loop and I'll let you know if it gets out of hand. Carry on!

See now, that's what we call a recipe for disaster. OK, not quite disaster, but that's definitely a recipe for inefficiency. What most people do not get is that a budget does not box employees in; it frees them up to do their jobs. If a budget is in place, everyone can use their brains and get the job done within the given parameters. Simple. Without a budget, the Cloudy Expectation land mine detonates and everyone stands around wondering why it's taking so long to get anything done.

Setting clear expectations and then sticking to them is one of the very bedrock qualities of leadership. The problem is, while too many people talk about this land mine, so few managers actually take the time and effort to articulate to their teams what their expectations are. The Cloudy Expectations land mine is a nasty one in that you only know you triggered it way after the fact. The cure is to get out in front of this one and to be on the lookout for every chance to make clear your expectations and then reinforce your leadership with unrelenting consistency.

Worth Repeating

- Lack of clear expectations often causes massive damage and delays.
- One of the most annoying features of this land mine is that when it's discovered it's maddening to see how easily it could have been avoided.
- It is a wise manager who sets very clear expectations on:
  - Conduct
  - Reporting and Feedback
  - Outcomes and Deliverables
  - Consequences
  - Budget.

chapter 7

Land Mine!
Confrontation Phobia

The Confrontation Phobia land mine … I believe I feel an analogy coming on. Yes, before we dive headlong into that nasty old Confrontation Phobia land mine, we must first consider this:

The Perfect Car, the Perfect Road, and the Steering Wheel

Visualize this picture with me now: You are outside on a beautiful day. You are standing next to a brand new car. It has never been driven, not one mile on it, and the wheels, suspension, alignment, and whatever have been perfectly calibrated. This is a perfect car. The road you are on is perfectly straight and perfectly flat. Can you see it?

You get in the car, start it up, put it in drive and floor the accelerator.

Perfectly aligned car. Perfectly straight road.

Here's the question: As you fly down the highway, are you or are you not going to have to put your hands on the steering wheel? Do you have to steer or can you leave your hands in your lap?

Of course, you have to steer. You never know what's going to happen down the road. Minor (and sometimes major) corrections and adjustments need to be made all along the way. If you don't steer, that car is eventually going to run off the road and cause nasty scrapes, dents, and possibly personal injury. That's just the way it is.

◻ ◻ ◻

So tell me, why do so many managers jump on the Confrontation Phobia land mine and leave their hands in their laps when they are supposed to be steering the car?

Driving safely requires that you steer the car. Leading the team properly requires that you confront issues when they arise. Simple as that. If you are a manager, this is the job they hired you to do.

The Confrontation Phobia land mine goes off whenever a manager chooses not to confront an issue because it's just plain easier to take the path of least resistance and let it go.

This is an ugly land mine. You have to take this one to heart because this ability to confront issues properly is at the very core of leadership. If nothing needed to be confronted, if everything worked smoothly, managers would not be needed. That's not the way it goes. In the professional world very little works smoothly, gets implemented perfectly, or arises without opposition. Confrontation is the business of meeting chal-

lenges big and small and managing through them. Unfortunately, too many managers avoid confrontation and in doing so
detonate the Confrontation Phobia land mine which eventually
has an extremely negative impact on their professional body of
work.

Confrontation itself tends to get a bad rap. When someone
says the word "confrontation," most people immediately have a
negative response. In fact, when a person is categorized as "confrontational," it usually means that person goes out of his or her
way to get in fights of one sort or another. Being labeled as "confrontational" is unfortunately not a compliment.

I stand on the other side of the debate table from most
people on this issue. I do not believe every confrontation has to be
negative or painful. In fact, once I realized that I was one of the
many who *avoided* confrontations, I made a decision never to shy
away from them and in so doing, I became a much better manager
and a much better leader.

Main Entry: con·front
Pronunciation: kon-front'
Function: transitive verb
1: to face, especially in challenge

The worst thing a manager can do is ignore a situation that
deserves to be confronted. I want you to erase from your managerial lexicon the phrase, "If I ignore it long enough, it'll go away."
Ignoring and avoiding situations that need to be confronted is an
extremely bad habit. And it's a slippery slope. Once you start
ignoring the situations and issues that need to be confronted, it
keeps getting easier and easier to do it because you eventually get
good at it. I've worked for a few bosses that were very good at

avoiding confrontation and they were a misery. Here's a story to illustrate. This story is called:

Tim Tobbogan
and the Commissions Dispute

A long time ago, I had a boss who was a career confrontation phobic. His name was certainly not Tim Toboggan, but for the purposes of this story, that's what I'm calling him. The book on Tim Toboggan was, given any decision point, he pretty much stayed on the fence and avoided any kind of confrontation. Actually, he never made a decision about much of anything unless he was forced into it, and as a rule, bobbed along like a cork on the ocean. The less involved he was, the better he liked it. The last thing this guy ever wanted was a confrontation, especially if that meant he had to make a decision on something.

This guy was a *branch manager*. He had like sixty-five people working for him. You cannot effectively run a team that size and avoid confrontations. And he didn't. He didn't *run* anything. He had the title that said he was the leader of the organization, but he *led* nothing. Eventually, the folks working in our branch office learned how to keep him out of the loop, get what they needed to get their own jobs done and let the chips fall where they may. If you ask me, I think he liked it that way. While this guy had a lot of leisure time, he was no leader. He made no contribution to our success and we knew it.

Tim unwittingly taught me an abrupt lesson about the dangers of not embracing confrontation. I was in a commission dispute and Tim had to decide between me and another sales manager who would get the full commission on a rather hefty sale. I booked an appointment with Tim and made my case on a

Tuesday afternoon. He responded to my argument very favorably, nodded in all the right places, and said things like, "Sounds good," and "That's the way I see it too." I walked out confident that I had won the issue and started mentally spending my next commission check, which was sure to be fat.

My rival in this dispute, who knew the lay of the land a bit better than I did at the time, walked into Tim's office late on Thursday afternoon, made his case and had the Tim-approved paperwork down to the commissions office that evening. My rival wins.

I lose.

No fat commissions check for Marty.

Game over. Please insert more tokens.

A rude awakening for me to be sure. I watched this and other dramas unfold and it became clear that whoever got to Tim last was going to win. So instead of us doing what was right for the business, we always wound up playing the "Who can be the last man in Tim's Office" game.

□   □   □

Tim Toboggan is not so much a great example of someone who simply avoided confrontation; rather he is a stellar example of someone who had made a *lifestyle* out of it. What's the point? The point is that Tim Toboggans are in no way an endangered corporate species, Tim Toboggans abound and none of them are leaders.

But what have we learned from Tim Toboggan vis-à-vis leadership? Well, I'll tell you what I learned, in a dispute there are always AT LEAST two sides to the story. As a leader, you have to know that, and you have to get both (or all) sides of a dispute before making your decision. And if Tim had just said "OK Mart, I hear you, but I'm not going to make a decision until I hear both sides of what's going on here" or *something* to that effect he'd have set my expectations appropriately. He would have exhibited leadership. That didn't happen and leadership did not play a part in Tim Toboggan's plan.

Now that was a situation where a manager was forced into making a decision. My rival and I approached Tim Toboggan and he had to react. Most management situations that deserve prudent and well-thought-out confrontation are usually more subtle and therefore easier to ignore.

I remember a situation I observed involving a few folks from our accounting group. The accounting group was a nice enough bunch headed up by a perfectly amiable young lady named Belinda. Belinda and the accounting group were responsible for keeping track of all office expenditures, managing our vendors, cutting travel and expense reimbursements, and producing the branch's monthly profit and loss reports.

Once a month, Belinda and the entire accounting group gathered in the conference room to participate in a conference call hosted by our Regional Finance Director. And thus begins a story called:

Belinda, Super Nerd, and the Overnight Envelope

One sunny October morning I popped into the conference room and found Belinda and the accounting team all gathered around the table. They had not yet dialed into the call and so I asked Belinda how long this kind of thing usually went because I was hoping to schedule the conference room as soon as she was through.

Before Belinda could answer me, one of her team members, a woman whom for the purposes of this story we will call Fetner, pointed at the phone and piped up with "Couldn't tell ya, Mart. Depends on how long Super Nerd keeps us."

The entire accounting team convulsed in laughter. I stood there thinking she'd respond to the rather derogatory comment made about her boss' boss, but even though Belinda looked a little unnerved by the comment, she said nothing. She had the chance to step in and show some leadership but since that would have necessitated a small confrontation, Belinda chose the Confrontation Phobia land mine instead.

I suppose she reasoned that since the call hadn't started yet, and since she was in Raleigh and her boss' boss, the Regional Finance Director, was in Atlanta, what harm could that kind of thing cause? She looked at me and said "Oh don't mind them. We should be done around 1:30." And so, I left.

Actually, at the time I did not give the incident another thought. Then, about three weeks later I got copied on an e-mail from somebody on our accounting team. The e-mail had very little to do with me and my team but I did notice that the author of the e-mail had openly referred to the Regional Director of Finance as Super Nerd. Uh oh. Seems that Fetner's little name for the Director had stuck and now all the kids in accounting were enjoying themselves. This was not my fight, it had nothing to do with me, but even from afar, I could tell that these guys were playing with fire.

And it was Belinda who got burned. Not more than a month later, someone else on Belinda's team sent an e-mail that referred to the Director of Finance as Super Nerd, that e-mail got answered, someone else got copied and around and around it went until finally somebody somewhere unwittingly copied the Director himself.

Whoops.

The next morning Belinda came into her office to find an overnight envelope from the Director sitting on her desk. The envelope contained the entire e-mail chain. The Regional Director of Finance for our company had taken the time to print it out and circle the numerous incidences that named him "Super Nerd" in red marker. On the top of the stack of paper, the Director had placed a note with a simple message that read, "Please call me immediately."

Ouch.

Oh Belinda. All you had to do was nip it in the bud. How hard would that have been? All you had to do was show a smidgen of leadership, confront the issue and make it clear to the team that this was unacceptable. But no. You ignored it. You figured it would go away. You stepped on the Confrontation Phobia land mine and the whole thing came back to bite you. One small confrontation would have saved you. A little leadership would have saved you. But you punked out, your career just took a serious hit. Sorry Belinda.

■   □   ▣

Think about it this way. Belinda had a choice, either she confronts the situation herself, or she herself gets confronted. Simple as that.

The Confrontation Phobia land mine isn't only dangerous when the confrontation is a reprimand or even laying down the law on an issue. Take late performance reviews for example. It has been my experience that delivering performance reviews late (or not at all) is some strange corporate disease. Even when a performance review should be delivered to a stellar employee, chances are the manager is late delivering it.

One issue is general laziness but I don't think that answers the whole question. I think the mystery component contributing to late performance reviews is confrontation phobia. It seems that even the whiff of a possible confrontation is enough to make some managers shy away.

Even during the most *positive* performance reviews when a raise is going to be handed out, some one-on-one coaching is expected, and that type of meeting has the potential for confrontation. My experience has been that employees are very hungry for coaching. When most people read their own performance reviews, they usually skip the praise and look for the parts where the boss has made recommendations for improvement. Most employees are *thankful* when a manager points out, professionally and with love, places where an employee needs to show some improvement. Good coaching usually deepens the respect and loyalty of an employee and that's why late performance reviews are a serious crime.

On my team, one extremely capable manager named Meredith was absolutely flawless in delivering performance reviews to her team on time. I asked her if she had made a conscious decision to keep her reviews on time or was this just part of her usual high-efficiency style.

> **MEREDITH:** Oh no! I have each one of my people marked on my calendar so I don't forget to do their review. Performance reviews are big.
>
> **MARTY:** Why do you think that is?
>
> **MEREDITH:** Um, performance reviews? I think it's like their birthday. No one drives to work, snaps their fingers

and says, "Oh yeah, today's my birthday!" Everybody knows when their birthday is.

MARTY: True enough.

MEREDITH: And everyone knows what month they should have their review. When is your next performance review due?

MARTY: February 12th.

MEREDITH: See? Also, it's a time when you and your boss sit down and talk about *you*. So most people not only know when it is, they look forward to it.

As usual, Meredith was right.

See, Meredith was beloved, but most of all she was respected because she was truly a leader. She was absolutely unafraid to confront any issue she felt had any material impact on her team or the business, and in doing so exhibited consistent leadership.

Avoiding the Confrontation Phobia Land Mine

Let's pull apart an actual situation in which I had every opportunity to ignore the opportunity to confront an issue but I did not. Don't get me wrong, I *thought* about ignoring it. I gave the "Ignore It and It'll Go Away" theory serious consideration. In the end though, I grew a backbone and made the right choice by meeting the issue head on.

The Employee Survey, Favorites, and the Eighth Floor

It was just another day in my insulated corporate world. There I was, in my office, bothering no one, when my trusted and invaluable administrative assistant, Doris, strolled into my office holding an ugly brown inter-office envelope.

> **MARTY (RECOILING IN FEAR):** What? What is that? Don't point that thing at me.
>
> **DORIS (SITTING DOWN AND HOLDING THE ENVELOPE ACROSS THE DESK):** It's from HR.
>
> **MARTY (HORRIFIED):** Aaaaaaah! No. No way. I'm out of town. I'm, um, I'm …
>
> **DORIS:** It's inter-office, Mart. C'mon, let's go, you know I'm not allowed to open this if it's addressed specifically to you.
>
> **MARTY:** Outpatient surgery! I'm having outpatient surgery! Torn rotator cuff! High ankle sprain! Irregular heartbeat! Deviated septum!!
>
> **DORIS (DROPPING THE ENVELOPE ON MY DESK):** Look, Marylynn from downstairs wants to make sure all the VP's get these.
>
> **MARTY:** Marylynn? Which one is Marylynn?
>
> **DORIS (NOT LOOKING BACK AS SHE WALKS OUT):** Marylynn. You said she has "Texas hair."
>
> **MARTY:** Oh, I know her. She's new.

Because I had been trained in unwinding the safety string thinger on the back of the interoffice envelope, I had the envelope opened in seconds. In no time, I had the contents of the envelope spread across my desk. My fear was for naught as I realized quickly that the envelope contained a summary of the responses to HR's giant employee satisfaction survey.

At first, I read the report only because I knew that if I read the thing I could later drop, in an off-handed manner, a quasi-relevant statistic from the survey while attending a high-level meeting. This would earn me valuable Company Man points with my superiors and greatly irritate my enemies. However, as I read the survey summary, one simple statistic leapt out at me. It turned out, according to the summary, 53 percent of the employees at World Headquarters answered that they felt "very strongly" that favoritism was an issue in our company. Favoritism. Hmm, that means salary increases, bonuses, and promotions were not handed out based on merit but based on who liked whom.

My initial thoughts were, and here we have a decision point, this is me deliberating so pay attention. My initial thoughts were:

> *"Well, obviously, not on the eighth floor. Not on <u>my</u> floor. Not <u>my</u> team. These guys know I love them all equally. Sure, they are each their own individual snowflake but I love them all equally. They all know that. Obviously none of <u>my</u> people answered with a "very strongly" on the favoritism question. That number's probably skewed by those social rejects down on the first floor. That's probably your answer right there. Yep."*

I was ready to leave it at that. Then I stopped. As easy as it would have been to ignore that survey and go along like always, I decided to dig into the situation. If my assumption was correct, then all was well. But it was an assumption. And if it turned out my team *did* think I was playing favorites, well now we have a problem. Time to take a little action and show a little leadership.

As soon as I decided to act I knew I was doing the right thing. So I yelled out of my office.

MARTY: Doris! Doris, my perfect angel.

DORIS: Oh please.

MARTY: C'mon in for two seconds.

DORIS (ARRIVING): What's up? I put the guys from legal on hold for this, so you can take your time.

MARTY: Who do we have out in the field and who's in the building?

DORIS: On *your* team?

MARTY: No, on the Chicago White Sox.

DORIS: Um, everyone's in the building except Large Settle. He's in Rocky Mount.

MARTY: Edgecombe County!

DORIS: Other than that, they're all here.

MARTY: OK, I want every one of them in the conference room at 4:45 today. Put the word out.

DORIS: Done. By the way, it's "whom."

MARTY: Whom what?

DORIS: It's "*Whom* do we have out in the field?" You said "who." It's "whom."

MARTY: You're fired.

DORIS: You wouldn't know the paperwork to get it done.

MARTY: Be gone from me. I cast you out as a demon.

And so it came to be that I stood before my assembled team in the conference room with the HR survey in my hand. I explained about the favoritism statistic. I told them that, while I didn't expect anyone to come forward right then, I wanted them to know I took this issue very seriously (which clearly, I did). I encouraged them to find me any time the next day, no questions asked, and let me know if they felt I was playing favorites and we could talk it over. It was rather a short gathering and again, I was keen to avoid melodrama. Still the message was sent.

◻ ◻ ◻

Beware the path of least resistance.

M. Clarke

The key is that I had every opportunity to ignore the survey. That would have been the path of least resistance to be sure. The point I want to make here is, as a manager, the path of least resistance is often your enemy. In fact, as a leader, I would assert that anytime you find yourself deciding what to do, or whether to do anything at all, beware the path of least resistance. That path is paved with undercurrents of resentments, petty jealousies, and lack of team harmony. Any manager who makes a habit of taking the path of least resistance is typically not going to last very long or rise very high.

In avoiding this very sneaky and destructive land mine, I encourage you to keep three rules of thumb in mind. And they are:

1. What you accept you teach.
2. Now is better than later.
3. Is that the hill you want to die on?

What you accept, you teach.

I do not know where my mother got hold of this phrase, but when she says, "What you accept, you teach," she is talking about avoiding the Confrontation Phobia land mine. Think about this for a second. As a manager, what you accept, you teach.

That means if you look the other way when you should confront poor performance, behavior, or general unrest, you are teaching everyone who reports to you that this performance, behavior, or unrest is perfectly OK.

Cast your thoughts back to poor Belinda. When she did not react, when she did not confront the issue when one of her employees referred to the Regional Director of Finance as Super Nerd, she taught her entire team that this was acceptable behavior. There's very little middle ground here. What you accept, you teach.

I saw a great bit of leadership that illustrates this point when I was visiting the great city of Knoxville, Tennessee. Knoxville! Home of the Volunteers and an airport recently redecorated in 1972. This story is called:

Harvey vs. Buster, "The Knoxville Showdown"

The situation was this: Knoxville was, for the most part, an underachieving sales office to say the least. This was not because the market was soft. Certainly not, Knoxville's a boom town! No, the reason that the Knoxville office never could get themselves above the quota line was because of Harvey.

Harvey was not only the Knoxville office's best sales person; he was the *company's* best sales person. He was number one and second place was an also ran. In the Knoxville sales office, it was Harvey radio: All Harvey, all the time. And Harvey knew it. Unfortunately, while Harvey's production was enough to make him a superstar, it was not enough to carry the whole sales office above the team quota.

Also, Harvey's sales numbers were huge but so was Harvey's attitude. Harvey didn't turn in sales reports. Harvey didn't go to sales meetings. Harvey's paperwork was always a mess because Harvey never did attend the training classes. Harvey was also a poison to the new recruits in Knoxville. He was forever running his mouth, spewing negativity to whomever was within earshot. All of this behavior was tolerated and never confronted by whatever sales manager happened to be occupying the Knoxville office at the time.

Why? Well Harvey himself had the answer: "I'm the best sales person in the company, you better not make me unhappy." Most managers, unfortunately, were just fine with that arrangement. Most of those Knoxville managers took the path of least resistance and in doing so immolated themselves on the Confrontation Phobia land mine.

The pattern that played out over four Knoxville sales managers in three years was this: Instead of confronting Harvey for his behavior, negativity, and general disregard for management, the sales manager would let Harvey go his own way, infecting all the other sales people and undermining the manager's authority in the process. And at the end of the month, typically Harvey would wind up 150 percent above quota and the Knoxville office as a group would end up at about 78 percent. This situation went on for years.

Until Harvey met Buster.

Buster was a young lady about 5' 3" tall, red hair, square jaw, pretty smile, and a backbone made of titanium. It took Buster about three days on the job to determine it was either confront Harvey and risk a possibly unpleasant situation or it was to knuckle under and eventually follow the other four failed managers out the door.

She'd been on the job about six months when I found myself back in the Knoxville sales office. The sales team had finally shown signs of life, had been above quota for two months and was looking very good for doing it again. I had to ask her how she did it. While we were eating lunch, the following conversation ensued:

MARTY: OK, let's have it.

BUSTER: What?

MARTY: The Knoxville office is number one in the region and number six in the company this month.

BUSTER: And we're going to be around number three next month.

MARTY: My point exactly. How'd you do it?

BUSTER: Well, you know, I think if you set goals, and don't expect your people to do anything you wouldn't do, you know, I guess the result …

MARTY: Harvey. What did you say to Harvey? I was in that sales meeting this morning, dear. Harvey didn't run his mouth at me once. Boy's had a personality transplant. Can tell by looking at him.

BUSTER: Harvey's having a great month.

MARTY: He was there on *time*. He didn't waltz in late with his usual strut and extra large double skinny latte with extra whip. Spare me the mom and apple pie. Did you, or did you not, straighten that kid out?

BUSTER (SMILING): Yes. Harvey and I had a conversation.

MARTY: When.

BUSTER: It was on the morning of my fourth day.

MARTY: No way.

BUSTER: Oh yeah, I could see how it was going to go with him. I mean I've seen it before. So I called him into my office and explained the situation to him.

MARTY: Explained the situation to him.

BUSTER: Sure, he was a little taken aback at first. I told him the specific behaviors that I was not going to tolerate any more and he tried to "Yeah, yeah, yeah" me.

MARTY: And what'd you do? Did you pull out your nunchakus and go all Jet Li on him?

BUSTER (LAUGHING): Nooo!

MARTY: I'd have had your back if you did.

BUSTER: No, no. Harvey sat in my office and tried to blow it all off and I just stood my ground and explained that my job was to get the Knoxville office performing above quota. And if he continued his whole Harvey act, if he continued to, you know, to hold himself above acting like a sales rep and being a source of negativity to my junior reps, then I'd let him go.

MARTY: You told him you'd fire him? Did he believe you?

BUSTER: I was *not* bluffing and I think he could tell. I mean, look at it, either we get the Harvey show or we get the entire Knoxville office up above quota. And that was that. I mean I didn't like *scream* at him, but I brought him up short and, well …

MARTY: Everything's great now.

BUSTER: Everything's *better*.

MARTY: Knoxville in the top five? Trust me that's great.

□　□　□

If Buster hadn't stepped in, if she had let Harvey continue his destructive, disrespectful ways, what message was she sending to the other reps and staff in the office? If she does not confront Harvey, she is de facto, *accepting* that behavior. That sends the message that the behavior is acceptable. What you accept, you teach. Confronting the behavior professionally and providing clear direction and a sense of the consequences of making another choice, is your route to true leadership. Ask yourself, what behavior are you accepting right now that you shouldn't?

Now is better than later (or Think, but think fast)

The Confrontation Phobia land mine is deadly but *speed* is its mortal enemy. Speed is by far your most important weapon in avoiding the Confrontation Phobia land mine. One of my favorite bosses, Tex, was the one who taught me that in any given managerial situation, the only thing that can hurt you is hesitation. My man Tex NEVER shied away from a necessary confrontation and he did so with amazing speed. His responses were well thought out and he moved on them quickly.

> *If it were done when 'tis done, then 'twere well*
> *It were done quickly.*
>
> W. SHAKESPEARE

Speed of reaction is critical in most leadership situations. As soon as your managerial intuition gives you a little tweak that something's not right, as soon as your mental "check engine" light comes on, pay attention to it and act as swiftly as you can.

Conversely, acting in a rash manner, or acting without thinking (the dreaded "knee-jerk"), often has pretty disastrous results too. So when you have to confront someone or some issue, *think*, but think fast. Here's a think-but-think-fast story called:

Jiffy, the Staff Meeting, and the Bathing Suit Comment

So there we were. Waaaaay up there in the ninth floor conference room, high atop World Headquarters. It was toward the end of the summer and I was holding an afternoon quarterly staff meeting. There were about twenty-one or twenty-two folks around the table. Marketing people, product managers, quality assurance, training, administrative staff, and public relations, all of us together.

Toward the end of the meeting, spirits were running high. These folks had all worked together for a number of years and were on excellent terms with each other. I forget who brought up the idea of a team pool party, but the idea gained immediate traction. Soon some of my more detail-oriented staff were deciding what dates were open, where we'd go, and who was to bring what.

I was most pleased. This was shaping up to be an epic party. Then, one of my product managers, a boy from Buffalo to whom, for his own protection, I'll refer to as Jiffy, went one step over the line. I had a choice either to let it go or address it. Here's how it went:

> **DELAWARE:** OK! OK! Ssshh. Everybody hush! OK, I have Large Settle bringing the caramel popcorn.
> **LARGE SETTLE:** Caramel popcorn. Got it. And I gotta buy a new swim suit. Old one's about wore out.

DELAWARE: That brings up a good point; nobody has to wear a bathing suit if you don't want to.

JIFFY: Yes they do! How else am I going to get to see Doris in a thong?

At this point, the entire table exploded into riotous laughter, Doris included. And well they should have, it was an extremely funny comment at the time.

Then, in the back of my head, I heard the voice whisper "Dangerrrr ... We're on thin ice here, Mart ..."

Because I often listen more closely to the voice in the back of my head than to the voices of the people around me, I stepped in and gingerly steered the discussion to a safer topic.

After the meeting, as I waited in the crowd for the elevator, I was deliberating on whether or not to confront Jiffy for his comment. On the one side, Doris was, and probably still is, as down to earth a person that you'll ever meet. She possesses a razor sharp sense of humor and indeed, she was laughing. On the other hand ... Because I've seen a few promising careers derailed, I have become hypersensitive to comments that flirt with the line between funny and inappropriate.

I figured I'd wait for the morning and see how I felt. Then, as the doors opened to let us on the elevator, I asked myself, "What would my old boss, Tex, do?" The answer was clear. Tex would be all over this and he'd be all over it right now. He wouldn't wait until tomorrow to confront the issue. Additionally the more I thought about it, the more I realized that by tomorrow, it would all be too late. I needed to act while the impact of that statement still hung in the air. I'd already blown the opportunity to confront the issue right as it happened. I turned to Jiffy in the elevator and said, "Jiff, come see me before you leave for the day."

And that was it. Alone in my office he and I talked it over, and he told me he "was just being funny" and that Doris "was cool" and would never go to Human Resources, I told him that was not the point. I told him that I just could not afford that kind of loose talk and if it happened again, *I'd* go to HR. That's just not the way I run the team.

Having had it explained to him that way, he was very receptive. Besides being a bit of a motor mouth Jiffy was, and probably still is a joy of an employee and a gifted product manager. He actually took it upon himself to approach Doris and make sure he hadn't offended her. The point is I acted then. That afternoon. Some situations can stand a bit of pondering. However, most benefit from thinking and acting quickly.

◻ ◻ ◻

Is that the hill you want to die on?

Not every situation, comment, or behavior needs to be confronted. If you tear off and confront every nit-picky thing, you become a micro-manager. This is the kiss of death. So to avoid becoming a micro-manager, the simple question, "Is this the hill you want to die on?" can be extremely useful in helping you decide where, when, and how to apply your efforts.

If you forget to ask yourself this question, sometimes you can get blinded to how your actions are affecting your team or even your own career. I heard a great story about a guy who absolutely left that question out of the equation, got himself "career-blind" and the results were catastrophic. I remember I was sitting on the edge of a huge pool when I heard this story.

The hub of social activity of the development in which my family and I reside is the giant community swimming pool. This thing is mammoth. In the summer months, it is not an unusual site to see about twelve million happy, screaming children in the pool. This leaves us, their parents, lining the outside of the pool, sitting on the ledge, dangling their feet in the water, and passing our summer afternoons and evenings talking about all things great and small.

Last summer I found myself sitting next to an excellent man about my age whom, for the purposes of this story I will refer to as Boris. Boris related an "Is that the hill you want to die on?" story to me called:

Renaldo, the White House, and the Parking Spot

Back in the late 90's my man Boris worked in Washington, DC. He was on staff in the President's administration and enjoyed the prestigious perk of having an office in the White House. He also informed me that this situation had, for almost all staffers, the unfortunate consequence of having to use methods of mass transit to commute to work every day. It seems that parking spaces at the White House are not in great supply. In fact, there are precious few of them and it is for this reason that every possible parking spot at the White House is assigned on the basis of rank.

Enter Renaldo. Renaldo was Boris' boss. Over time, he had clawed his way up the ranks of the President's administration to the point where Renaldo had reached the lofty position of Anonymous Government Functionary. Since he had a few people reporting to him, that meant he was management! This, in Renaldo's mind, meant he got a parking space.

153

As Boris tells it, at first Renaldo tried dropping hints to his superiors that he would like, and owing to his diligently acquired rank, he was *due*, an assigned parking space of his very own. His hints did not fall on deaf ears but he was denied. Actually, he was never flat out denied, he just never got his spot from the powers that be. This was when Renaldo started thinking very small. The parking spot issue started to consume him and his thoughts. His issues were:

1. I am *entitled* to a parking space.
2. I shouldn't have to *beg* for a parking space.

See? That was the problem: Renaldo was right. He was in the right and he knew it and this gave Renaldo a scorching case of righteous indignation. And, as we all know, righteous indignation is the enemy of clear thinking and the warm friend of petty, small-minded petulance. Renaldo's indignant rage burned slowly, fueled every day by the uncertainty surrounding the question of who exactly gave out these spots? Renaldo reasoned that if he could just figure out who had the authority to grant him his parking spot, he'd make his case to that person and he'd soon be pulling up to the guard gate, flashing his permit, and pulling into his very own parking spot. He'd walk to work with his head held high as his car cooled in the shadow of the White House complex.

So of course, Renaldo never shut up about it. I am not sure what the precise statistic is, I have no clue what the actual head count of the Commander in Chief's staff is, but since it takes two buildings besides the White House itself to house these folks every day, well I imagine the number is pretty healthy.

Renaldo left no stone unturned. He asked everyone he could think of about the parking issue. As you might expect, Boris said it got to be rather a joke up and down the corridors of the administration buildings. However, Renaldo was not to be denied.

He brought out the big guns by putting his request in writing. Uh oh. Not only did he make a formal request on letterhead, but also in the request, he listed all his efforts to be assigned a parking spot and made some recommendations that the process be a bit clearer in the future.

Well, that memo got forwarded up and up the chain of command. Renaldo was very much on top of the progress his request was making and every time it looked like progress had stalled, Renaldo was there to move it along. Have to admit, the boy was focused. The memo eventually made it onto the desk of the President's Chief of Staff.

Now here's me, sitting on the side of the community pool in my Myrtle Beach '98 t-shirt with my legs in the water and my mouth gaping at Boris as he told me that.

> MARTY (RECOVERING): That is such a lie. No way was the Chief of Staff involved.
>
> BORIS (SMILING): Nope, it's true. Why would I lie? I'm telling you the Chief of Staff had the memo on his desk. It is absolutely true.
>
> MARTY: A parking spot.
>
> BORIS: Yep. That's why the story is so *funny*. It's funny because it's true.

Now, I do not consider myself completely vacant of political acumen but truth to tell, when I think of the items that might be on the to-do list of the President's Chief of Staff I think of things like:

- The safety and well being of the American people
- The economy
- Health care
- Foreign policy
- The state of the union address or whatever.

You get the point. And while that list may not be entirely accurate and complete, the point is the Chief of Staff has some big fish to fry on a daily basis and here, plunked on his desk, is Renaldo's memo. Let the games begin.

The memo came rocketing back down the chain of command and what do you know, Renaldo got his parking spot. By order of the President's Chief of Staff, Renaldo got his spot, his badge, the whole shootin' match.

So Renaldo wins, right? No, my perfect friends, Renaldo loses.

Think about it. Because the parking spot was the hill upon which Renaldo was apparently willing to die, everyone from the lowest rank possible all the way up to the Chief of Staff knew that the biggest issue for Renaldo over the last seven weeks was *not* a matter of national interest; it was a parking spot. So even if they didn't even *know* the guy, what is their opinion of Renaldo?

Yes, "Renaldo is a small-minded dope" is the correct answer. His superiors thought that way and Renaldo's own staff knew it too.

MARTY: Was he a genuinely dumb guy?
BORIS: No! He was a bright person. And a decent manager. But that whole thing just sunk the guy. I mean,

Renaldo lets it go and rides the Metro with the rest of us and he'd have lasted a lot longer.

MARTY: They fired him?

BORIS: Oh yeah. Six months later, they canned him. No joke. I forget why they said. But we all knew, you know?

MARTY: That is an incredible story.

BORIS: I know. Can't make that kind of thing up.

□　□　□

Poor Renaldo. *Qué lástima*. Had he just stopped and asked himself, OK, is this the hill I want to die on? He may have snapped out of it. Who knows what would have happened but he wouldn't have embarrassed himself in front of his superiors and his staff.

So what situations do you confront and which ones do you let go? In Renaldo's case, it was obvious to everyone but Renaldo. Going to bat for seven straight weeks for a parking spot is small-minded any way you slice it. Plain as day. Unfortunately, the situations that come to a leader's attention are often a lot less clearly defined. Still, the question needs to be asked and it can only be answered by the leader himself or herself.

Typically, when you ask yourself, "Is this the hill I want to die on?" about a particular issue, you can use the following three guidelines in order to help you make the best decision for yourself, your team, and the company. These guidelines have helped me immensely.

Guideline #1: Is it good for business?

So many times when you are immersed in an issue or one comes out of nowhere and blindsides you, you can lose perspective. You lose sight of the big picture and/or the core business results you and your team are trying to achieve.

Once you ask yourself this question and answer with cruel honesty, you can separate yourself from the situation itself, emotionally disengage and begin to make well-thought-out decisions that will be in the best interest of the business.

Guideline #2: Is it consistent with my pattern?

Again, think in terms of your leadership body of work. If you cannot identify your pattern of behavior and leadership responses, that's not tragic. Now is the time to start thinking about establishing your pattern of behavior. Consistency is a huge cornerstone in the leadership edifice.

If you *are* a consistent manager, then ask yourself while thinking (quickly) about a possible confrontation whether or not your course of action is consistent with that pattern. If it is consistent, then your actions will be in line with what you stand for and what you will and will not tolerate, thus reinforcing and adding to your leadership body of work.

If your actions break your pattern, are you doing that by design? Trying to effect some change? Inconsistency is not necessarily a bad thing if done sparingly and purposefully to effect positive change.

Guideline #3: Do I have my reasons worked out in my head?

As I have stated, I encourage one and all to think and think quickly. Please note that I use the phrase "worked out in my head" rather than "*perfected* in my head." As long as you can get your mental arms around a possible confrontation and see in your mind what the probable consequences of your actions will be, then go ahead and act.

Let's apply these three rules of thumb to two of the scenarios I've used in this chapter.

Scenario: Jiffy makes an inappropriate remark in a meeting.
Question: Do I confront him?

Is confronting the issue good for business? Yes. If I let it go, I'm inviting more of that type of behavior. Plus, if someone did make a complaint later, it would only serve as a distraction to me, the principals in the complaint, and my entire staff. I am inclined to confront Jiffy on this.

Is it consistent with my pattern? Yes. I have a pretty low tolerance for any kind of toe-over-the-line comments. For whatever reason, I have a heightened sensitivity. So yes, I have a history of being rigid on the issue.

Do I have my reasons worked out in my head? Yes. I need to get this nipped in the bud. I cannot let him slide. This alone will send the message I want to send to my team.
Answer: Confront Jiff before he leaves for the day.

Scenario: Renaldo wants his parking spot.
Question: Does he confront the issue?

Is confronting the issue good for business? No. It's not bad for business, but it has nothing to do with the results he was trying to accomplish with his staff.

Is it consistent with my pattern? No. According to Boris, Renaldo usually had things pretty well thought out and was on his way to bigger and better things in the administration. For some reason, he had a blind spot on the parking issue.

Do I have my reasons worked out in my head? We'll never know. I suspect if Renaldo ever checked himself and asked, "Where am I going with this whole parking spot thing?" he'd have realized that he was creating a tempest in a teacup. An annoying and credibility killing tempest.

Answer: Leave the parking spot issue alone.

Even though tripping the Confrontation Phobia land mine and deciding to head down the path of least resistance feels great in the short term, those types of decisions are surely the ones that hurt you in the long run. These are the moves that hurt your professional body of work. What kind of pattern of behavior are you looking to establish? Certainly, you want to be counted upon by your team and your superiors to be well-thought-out and able to make the decisions that help the business. Most times, establishing this pattern of behavior is going to rule out the path of least resistance and help you ascend into the very valuable role as a leader.

Worth Repeating

- Confronting issues properly as they arise is at the very core of effective leadership.
- Beware the path of least resistance.
- Remember these three rules of thumb when deliberating whether or not to confront an issue:
  - What you accept you teach
  - Now is better than later
  - Is that the hill you want to die on?
- As for, "Is this the hill you want to die on?" ask yourself these three questions to help you arrive at an appropriate answer:
  - Is it good for business?
  - Is it consistent with my pattern?
  - Do I have my reasons worked out in my head?

chapter 8

Land Mine!

Managing by Committee

The Managing by Committee land mine is a leadership deficiency so common it defies measurement by conventional mathematics.

This land mine detonates any time progress on a project slows down, or a critical decision gets delayed or never gets made at all because someone, somewhere down the line decides that he or she does not want to shoulder the responsibility of being entirely accountable.

Managing by committee spreads the accountability around, thus mitigating the chances that the manager will end up standing alone with his or her decision, shouldering all the accountability himself or herself. That thought can be a bit intimidating. But remember: Lonely is part of the job. Do not fear it and do not manage around it.

The Managing by Committee land mine goes off every time an employee in a leadership position looks accountability in the face, and quietly runs in the opposite direction to find a crowd into which he or she can disappear.

If a person in a leadership position waited for everyone to come to perfect agreement before actually doing anything of any weight, that person would never do anything of any weight. That person would never lead anything or anyone. Take a look around and try to identify projects and initiatives that are stalled or just plain dead because no one is taking a leadership position, staking themselves out, and making decisions.

But Mart, what about being a team player?

Don't we need everyone on the same page?

C'mon, don't we need everyone singing from the same hymnal?

For progress to occur, at some point somebody (let's just hope it's the individual in the leadership position), is going to step up and say, "OK, I hear what you have to say. Now here's the way we're going on this."

That's it. That's leadership. It sounds like this: "Here's my decision and if it turns out to be a disastrous failure, I'm accountable. But this is the direction, this is the decision, this is the way we're going folks. The train has just left the station."

Now that may sound easy to do, but you would not believe how many professionals avoid that type of accountability like it was radioactive or something.

Here, let me relate an actual story where the Managing by Committee land mine went off in a big way. This story is called:

Elroy, GodzillaCom, and the Animation Project

I don't know if you've ever been to an extremely large industry trade show, but I have and let me tell you, these things are impressive. In fact, some of them are so huge that there are only a few cities in the world that can accommodate their magnitude. No joke. In America, once you get into a certain category of number of attendees and companies exhibiting, you have a very slim selection of cities that have the capability to house the event and accommodate the mobs of people who attend and work the show.

To the uninitiated, these trade shows appear to be a colossal waste of time and every one who goes just parties a lot and sleeps late for days.

Not so.

In fact, back in the day, at my midsize telecommunications company about 18 percent of our annual gross revenue was won or lost during the six trade shows at which we exhibited. Safe to say, a lot of money was on the line at each one, and we took those shows pretty seriously.

Back then, the biggest trade show in my industry took place in Atlanta, Georgia. For the sake of illustration, let's just call it GodzillaCom. GodzillaCom gathered to itself every telecommunications carrier, vendor, equipment manufacturer, and major bandwidth consumer in North America.

It was huuuuge. In fact, the trade show booths erected at GodzillaCom had more square footage and were actually better appointed than my first house. The companies that sponsored those booths were hoping to make a seriously big impression on the attendees, an impression that could translate into revenue.

As Vice President of Marketing, my department was responsible for making sure that our booth, our exhibits, and our staff projected the absolute best possible impression of our company during these events. And so, about seventy-five days before GodzillaCom, I was summoned to my President's office.

REX: Mart, can I just tell you I love our trade show booth? Can I just tell you that?

MARTY: I'm glad you're pleased.

REX (LEANING BACK IN CHAIR AND LOOKING AT THE CEILING): Well, we gotta build on that, Mart. We gotta, you know, we gotta …

MARTY: Leverage our advantage.

REX (SNAPPING BACK TO ATTENTION): What? Where'd you learn that?

MARTY: I read it in a magazine.

REX: I don't pay you to read, Mart. OK? Cancel your subscription to whatever you read that in. OK?

MARTY: OK.

REX: What were we talking about? You made me lose my place.

MARTY: The trade show—

REX: The trade show booth! A thing of beauty. Man, I love that thing, but we need an animated video! Those boys in the Carrier division are right. We're like the only company without animated video. We're lookin' bad.

MARTY: Animation.

REX (HANDS WAVING AROUND OVER HIS HEAD): Yeah, like an animated, computer-generated video that comes on and shows off our giant network. I had this idea where it could be designed so you had the point of view of an actual bit of data and you go whizzing around our network. You're a bit traveling in our network and … Like you're just screaming along, right? And it shows that we have network everywhere, Mart. Like we have network in East Bend. Who has network in East Bend?

MARTY: Yadkin County!

REX: See? See my point? OK, so like ... what? 30 seconds? 45 seconds? Whatever. But like on a loop so people see it and they get drawn into our booth.

MARTY: On the video screens.

REX: Mart, what am I talking about here? Yes. On the video screens. You on this or what?

MARTY: We're gonna need this by GodzillaCom.

REX: Mart! If we have it after G-Com, what good does it do us?

MARTY: I'm on it.

REX: I know you're on it, Mart, but I'm talking over here and you're lookin' at me like a dog watchin' television my man.

MARTY: No, I have it.

REX: Like you're seein' me, and you're hearin' me ...

MARTY: I'm on it.

REX: But you're juuuuuuust not getting me. Who you gonna put on this?

MARTY: Um, I'm gonna put Elroy on this one. He's done the most work with the Carrier division.

REX: Know what? I don't care. I'm gonna be in Atlanta, I'm gonna be at GodzillaCom and I expect some serious animation attracting people to my booth.

MARTY: I got it. We won't disappoint you.

REX (TURNING HIS BACK TO ME SO HE CAN READ HIS E-MAIL): You never do, my man. You never do.

A word about "the Carrier division." The Carrier division was comprised of about twelve or so folks down on the second floor who sold, managed, and serviced our largest clients. As a group, they accounted for 60 percent of the company's revenue. The problem was they knew it. They knew it and they acted like it. A demanding and opinionated bunch to say the least. But they delivered. I'll give them that. So we tried to keep them happy (within reason anyway).

After I got through with Rex, I went downstairs and I laid it all out for Elroy. We had seventy-five days before GodzillaCom. Within those seventy-five days, we had to go from zero to delivery. No small order, but I was confident that Elroy was up to it. After all, he was an extremely reliable young man and he could pick up this project and run with it.

Well, I knew he was capable, but I found out the hard way that capability and leadership are two different skill sets. My boy Elroy was a tad short on the latter.

Over the next two months, Elroy was going along great. He had contacted a local graphics company and had them working on the project. Every ten days or so he had me sit in for a few looks at their demos and we made changes and edits. On three other occasions we showed demos to the Carrier division manager and to my boss, Spike. They both gave extremely insightful suggestions about changes that should be made, and we followed them to the letter. I was feeling very good.

But then, a scant two weeks before GodzillCom, two weeks before the entire Carrier division and the executive team traveled to Atlanta to stand in the booth under those video screens, shake hands, meet with clients and prospects, and hopefully lock up signatures on very significant revenue, Elroy decided to jump on the

Managing by Committee land mine. When it went off, it caused us both a lot of heartache, and unfortunately, it lowered Elroy's stock price in my mind.

On this occasion, Elroy lit the fuse of the Managing by Committee land mine with a simple e-mail message. I remember sitting at my desk, thinking up bold strategies and dreaming up creative initiatives, when I saw I had a new e-mail message from Elroy. My heart sank a bit when I read the subject line, "Trade Show Booth Animation Preview!" My heart sank entirely through my stomach and down into the liquid magma of our mother earth when I saw he'd invited not only the entire marketing team, the executive team, the entire Carrier division, but also a few select misfits from departments that had little or nothing to do with GodzillaCom.

Oh no. Oh, Elroy, we were so close.

My phone rang and shocked me out of my malaise. When I saw who was calling me I was shocked past malaise and into full panic. It was my boss, Spike.

Maybe I was wrong. Maybe he hadn't seen the message yet. Maybe he had seen it and didn't care. Perhaps I was overreacting. Perhaps Spike was calling me to go get his Porsche washed. A menial task to be sure, but a welcome one at this point because the most intelligent part of my brain was saying, "RUN! Flee the building! Run Marty boy and go get a job as a carnie. Carnies don't have these problems! Carnies just put together Ferris wheels! RUN!"

Contrary to my pathetic hopes, being sent to get Spike's Porsche washed or working the Ferris wheel as a carnie never evinced themselves as options during my phone conversation with Spike.

Marty: Hiya boss!

Spike: You read your e-mail yet?

Marty: Um, well, is this about—

Spike: What is on that kid's MIND?

Marty: Spike, this is not a big deal. I don't think anyone's actually going to show up anyway.

Spike: You better hope. What was he THINKING? We're gonna have a roomful of people telling us what's wrong with the project and you KNOW this is going to put us right back to square one.

Marty: Are you going?

Spike: No I'm not going. All I need is those Carrier yahoos telling me their opinion. No, I am not going.

Marty: Well that's good because neither am—

Spike: Because YOU'RE going. You go and take notes and nod and do what you do. This is ridiculous. And in the future, you better put that kid on a short leash.

Marty: I'll be there. After the meeting, you want me to circle back with you?

Spike: No.

I was wrong about one thing: That meeting was *very* well attended. Elroy unveiled his project not only in front of the groups he invited, but also in front of some other folks who figured they'd better drop by just to bless us all with their valuable insights. It was a mess.

There we were, about seven million of us packed into the fifth floor conference room. Elroy played the animation on the big screen for everyone. When it was over, the entire audience applauded. I was way in the back of the room and when I heard that applause, a temporary wave of relief washed over me.

I use the adjective "temporary" here because my relief was extremely short-lived. Once the applause died down, the big buts came out and I knew we were doomed.

Elroy, fabulous job. I love it, BUT ...

Listen, I don't know anything about computer-generated stuff or whatever, BUT ...

That one part in the beginning is awesome, BUT ...

And so it went for about 45 minutes. That smiling group of corporate sharks just savaged my boy Elroy. After they'd finished feasting on his self-esteem, they drifted away, leaving nothing but scorched earth where Elroy once stood. I almost felt sorry for him. Then I remembered, bitterly, that he asked for it with that stupid e-mail and now we were all either:

A. Back to square one like Spike said, or
B. In a position to plainly ignore the opinions that surfaced in a meeting specifically called for the purpose of gathering opinions.

Elroy caved under the weight of the prospect of leadership and fooled himself into thinking he was doing the right thing by trying to manage his project by committee. Eventually I had to step in and make the decision that we would indeed go with the animation as it stood because:

A. It would have doubled the cost to make the changes suggested in the meeting and
B. Those changes would have taken us a whole lot more time than the two weeks we had until GodzillaCom.

In Atlanta, when the animation loop ran on the video screens as planned, our customers and prospects loved it. Typically,

I would have enjoyed my department's successful delivery of such a high-profile project. But I didn't enjoy those few days in Atlanta simply because for the entire show the Carrier folks rained their murderous barbs and snide comments down upon us. We had wasted their time. Why did we hold the meeting if we weren't going to change anything? Even though I told most of them to button it, they did have a point and I admit I was very relieved when GodzillaCom was over.

◻   ◻   ◻

Now let's examine Elroy's motives for inviting the known world to cast opinions on his project just two weeks before it was supposed to go live. I questioned the boy myself on the matter and after I heard him out, it all came down to this: The Carrier group was an opinionated bunch and he didn't want to take the heat if they didn't like what they saw when the animation was unveiled at GodzillaCom.

That was about it. He had his boss' buy-in, and his boss' boss' buy-in. He even had the Carrier department head on board. Perfect. Truth be told, the animation was very cool and was going to reflect extremely well on my company. Still you cannot please everyone, and there was no way Elroy was going to Atlanta and stand in the fire when those Carrier folks started punching holes in his work. He was intimidated by that scenario and he indulged his fear instead of stepping up to it. Simple as that.

As you can see, the Managing by Committee land mine usually detonates because of fear of accountability. Accountability is the bedrock of leadership and sometimes it's a scary proposition. Sometimes it may look like you're going to have to stand in the fire alone while the results of your decisions and actions get played out in front of you for all to see.

When you feel that intimidation, when you feel that fear, it's good news because you are at the leadership crossroads. As far as that decision point is concerned, your next move will define you and the power to demonstrate leadership is in your hands.

Avoiding the Managing by Committee Land Mine

I want to arm you with two rules of thumb that you can use to avoid this terrible leadership land mine. And they are:

1. There's a difference between a vote and a say.
2. Show a little backbone.

A vote vs. a say

I have latched onto a nine word sentence that has guided me past some very complex situations, and always keeps me safe from triggering the Managing by Committee land mine. I don't know where I heard this. It's entirely possible I made it up myself. In any event, I pass it along to you and I encourage you to keep this sentence at the ready for yourself:

There's a difference between a vote and a say.

Oooooh yes. This one's very close to my heart. I find myself leaning on this phrase often, whether I'm counseling an executive team or coaching an individual. Even my children understand this phrase because I find it valuable in parenting.

When I was the leader of sizeable departments, I explained that sentence to my team many, many times. Often when we'd be working to come up with a new marketing campaign or a training project the time would come to make a decision and make some material progress. Keep in mind, I employed some extremely creative and capable people; they all had a personal stake in their ideas getting implemented. Usually, when the dust settled, we were left with many good and inventive ideas.

Then the lobbying would begin. With all these good ideas, which way are we going to go? Which idea wins? In the ensuing melee alliances would form. Old grudges would reemerge. Points would be argued. Agendas would be hidden or at least thinly veiled. What a fracas.

At times, I'd participate in the debate, but mostly I'd use my two ears in proportion to my one mouth. Sure enough, eventually it would come down to me to make the decision on which direction we'd take and I would remind my team, "OK, there's a difference between a vote and a say. I hired you because you're smart and I want to hear your vote. So let's go around the horn one more time here, and then I'll make a decision on how we're going to proceed. There's a difference between a vote and a say. I'm the say."

My team understood this and they didn't resent it in the slightest for two reasons:

1. In a complicated situation, it comes as a *relief* to the team for the ranking person in the room to exercise some authority.
2. My team knew with them I was the say, but in my own boss' office, I just had a vote and that's the way of the world.

Show a little backbone

Anyone in a leadership position is going to be faced daily with the responsibility of making decisions. Many of these decisions require that leader to show a little backbone, to stand in the fire, pick the aphorism of your choice. The seat of leadership is no place for the weak-willed.

Oh, the Managing by Committee land mine is seductive because it plays right on that fear of opposition. However, if you see it coming you can gear your head up for it and take it like a leader. And it's *going* to happen. Believe it. So don't get all bunched up and cave in when it happens.

Because once you decide on a course of action, announce it, and essentially stake yourself out, there's no turning back. Well, actually, there's plenty of turning back but it can be catastrophic to your credibility to cave in and reverse field. Here's a quick story to illustrate.

Emily and the New Compensation Plan

Emily was VP of sales over five area managers and fifty sales reps. After a few agonizing weeks of crunching numbers, Emily realized that she needed to restructure how some of the sales got counted and who got credit for what. This was going to pay some people more and some people less, but finally the sales team was going to be compensated correctly and this would, she surmised, lead to more motivated employees and even bigger sales revenues. Most importantly, this was the exactly correct thing to do in terms of the company's financial health.

The company was five years old at the time and this was going to be the first time the organization had changed the compensation plan. Any way she sliced it, the new system made much more sense for the entire company and, given a little time, would be a huge success. While Emily knew this plan would please some sales reps, she knew she was going to hear some serious opposition from some others.

So Emily announced her decision with the full backing of the executive team. And just as she predicted, the reps who had been getting fat off the old compensation plan went bats. Opposition was immediate and it was furious. One guy actually did announce he was quitting but kept coming to work anyway. Other than that, it was all phone calls, e-mails, and conversation. It was all noise.

I know you don't want to hear this but after a few days, Emily caved. She did not stand in the fire and in less than a week, the noise got to her and the change in compensation was never instituted—the company continued its poor financial performance.

◻ ◻ ◻

Now, you tell me, what message did Emily send to everyone familiar with the situation? Correct! She sent the message that if you complain, if you make enough noise, she'll cave in and let the situation be managed by committee. In this case, the committee was her and the entire sales team. Like most situations that get managed by committee, a good decision got lost and the company suffered.

Listen, you are *going* to be faced with decisions that pit what you know is right for the company against your fear of taking some heat in the process.

Heat.
Opposition.
Pushback.
Flack.
Lip.

It's all the same and here's a secret: it's all noise. I cannot tell you how many leaders live in fear of the above list, but it's all just noise.

> *They can yell at you, but they can't eat you.*
>
> R. WATRAL

I've made many decisions that turned out to be correct and prudent but, when I made them, engendered no small amount of heat from my peers and my own team. But it was all noise. Never once in my professional life did anyone actually take a bite out of me because of a decision I made. No one took a swing at me. No one threw rocks at me.

So, what's the moral of the story? The moral of the story is that showing a little backbone is actually *easier* than you think. There's nothing to fear. They can't eat you.

The first order of business is raising your awareness to this land mine. When you see it (and you will) I want you to be the one who can take a stand, make a decision, and accept accountability. Even though you cannot operate in a vacuum, and input is an essential component to every sound decision, eventually, you're either going to stand by your decisions and act like a leader, lonely as that may be, or you're going to sacrifice your leadership for the sake of the warmth of the crowd.

Worth Repeating

- Sometimes lonely is part of the job.
- There's a difference between a vote and a say. If you want to emerge as a leader, you must accept that in the end, you are the say.
- Show a little backbone.
- Do not fear the noise. They can yell at you but they can't eat you.

OK, Now What?

Let's get the eight leadership land mines out in front of us for the purposes of review, shall we?

Managing the Situation
- It's All about Me
- Managing to the Exception
- The Super Doer
- The Blame Addiction

Leading Your People
- The Popularity Priority
- Cloudy Expectations
- Confrontation Phobia
- Managing by Committee

Keep these leadership land mines in front of you. Burn them onto your mental C drive and never lose sight of them. These are specific behaviors that cripple your ability to lead effectively. Just being mindful of them will make it easier for you to avoid them.

Remember: Leadership is not an event; it's a *lifestyle*.

Keep in mind how we started: *Think "body of work."* You will continue to face countless decision points as you navigate through your professional days and weeks. Each decision you make is an opportunity either to jump on and suffer the damage of a leadership land mine, or a chance to avoid the leadership land mines, and in so doing enhance your professional body of work and emerge as a true leader.

Going forward, your consistency and your conviction are your most powerful assets. Keep your head and your heart in the game. Keep your eyes open, pay attention and above all, *think!* It's all about the decision points. What you do, what you say, how you act, all of this impacts not only yourself but also the lives and livelihoods of your people.

I know you'll make the right decisions. Good luck, and remember I'm rooting for you.

Like the book?
You'll love it live!

Marty Clarke is an internationally recognized professional speaker and can deliver his *Leadership Land Mines* keynote for your organization. But keep in mind …

Just for the record:

QUESTION: Can Marty's presentation be customized?

ANSWER: Absolutely.

QUESTION: Will Marty behave himself?

ANSWER: Certainly not.

For all booking information go to

www.martyclarke.com